Mathematics for Every Student

Responding to Diversity,
Grades 9–12

Mathematics for Every Student

A series edited by Carol E. Malloy

Mathematics for Every Student
Responding to Diversity,
Grades 9–12

Volume Editor

Alfinio Flores
University of Delaware
Newark, Delaware

Series Editor

Carol E. Malloy
University of North Carolina at Chapel Hill
Chapel Hill, North Carolina

NATIONAL COUNCIL OF
TEACHERS OF MATHEMATICS

Copyright © 2009 by
THE NATIONAL COUNCIL OF TEACHERS OF MATHEMATICS, INC.
1906 Association Drive, Reston, VA 20191-1502
(703) 620-9840; (800) 235-7566; www.nctm.org
All rights reserved

Library of Congress Cataloging-in-Publication Data

Mathematics for every student. Responding to diversity, grades 9–12 / volume editor, Alfino Flores.
    p. cm. (Mathematics for every student)
  ISBN 978-0-87353-613-4
  1. Mathematics—Study and teaching (Secondary) —United States. 2. Multicultural education—
United States. 3. Educational equalization—United States. I. Flores, Alfino. II. Title: Responding to diversity,
grades 9–12.
  QA13.M35452 2009
  510.71'273—dc22

                    2008041742

The National Council of Teachers of Mathematics is a public voice of mathematics education,
providing vision, leadership, and professional development to support teachers in ensuring
equitable mathematics learning of the highest quality for all students.

Printed in the United States of America

Contents

Contents—*Continued*

The National Council of Teachers of Mathematics (NCTM) has demonstrated its dedication to equity in the mathematics education of *all students* through its publications, through regional and annual meeting programs, and through professional development programs. In clarification of what is meant by *all students*, in 1990 the NCTM Board of Directors endorsed the following statement, which set the mathematical education of every child as the goal for mathematics teaching at all levels.

> As a professional organization and as individuals within that organization, the Board of Directors sees the comprehensive mathematics education of every child as its most compelling goal.
>
> By "every child" we mean specifically—
>
> - students who have been denied access in any way to educational opportunities as well as those who have not;
>
> - students who are African American, Hispanic, American Indian, and other minorities as well as those who are considered to be a part of the majority;
>
> - students who are female as well as those who are male; and
>
> - students who have not been successful in school and in mathematics as well as those who have been successful.
>
> It is essential that schools and communities accept the goal of mathematical education for every child. However, this does not mean that every child will have the same interests or capabilities in mathematics. It does mean that we will have to examine our fundamental expectations about what children can learn and can do and that we will have to strive to create learning environments in which raised expectations for children can be met. (NCTM 1991, p. 4)

Through the Equity Principle in *Principles and Standards for School Mathematics* (2000), NCTM built on the challenging goal of the "every child" statement above and extended its vision of equity by stating, "Excellence in mathematics education requires equity—high expectations and strong support for all students" (p. 12). Specifically, the principle states that equity requires high expectations and worthwhile opportunities for all, requires accommodating differences to help everyone learn mathematics, and requires resources and support for all classrooms and all students (pp. 12–14). Guided by the Equity Principle and the charge of the NCTM Educational Materials Committee, the editors of this three-book series are pleased to feature instructional practices of teachers from diverse classrooms that embody this principle and the "every child" statement.

The editors would like to thank the authors, who were willing to share their experiences and successful strategies for teaching all students in diverse classrooms; the numerous reviewers for their contributions; and the NCTM Publications Department for their support, patience, and encouragement from our initial meeting through the publication phases of this project. I personally want to thank the volume editors, who worked tirelessly during the development of this series. It was a pleasure and an intellectual inspiration to work with them. They were my friends, critics, and colleagues.

—*Carol E. Malloy*
Series Editor

REFERENCES

National Council of Teachers of Mathematics (NCTM). *Professional Standards for Teaching Mathematics*. Reston, Va.: NCTM, 1991.

———. *Principles and Standards for School Mathematics*. Reston, Va.: NCTM, 2000.

Introduction

WE ARE teachers, teachers of mathematics. Every year we are excited to meet the new students who are placed in our classrooms to learn about mathematics. On the first day of school as we look around the room at their faces, we know that every student has the ability to learn mathematics. At the same time students look to our faces for guidance through the mathematics content and to their mathematical understanding. Students' confidence in our skills is both our inspiration and our challenge, especially because we know, as Bobbie Poole stated in *I Am a Teacher* (Marquis and Sachs 1990, p. 20),

> Every kid is different. What's exciting is to try to meet the needs of those individual kids. It is never boring. It is different from minute to minute, and there is no formula that works for everyone.

Knowing that no one strategy will work for all students, teachers have the responsibility to determine strategies, both affective and cognitive, that together support all students as they learn mathematics. Affective behaviors—which include students' beliefs about mathematics and self, teachers' beliefs, and students' emotions and attitudes—play a prominent role in achievement (McLeod 1991). In the vignette that follows, I describe a situation that I experienced with a student, Alfred, who because of lack of confidence in his academic skills was a behavioral challenge in my mathematics class.

Teachers have the responsibility to determine strategies, both affective and cognitive, that together support all students as they learn mathematics.

Building Confidence through Caring

In my sixth year of teaching, my husband and I moved to a city where he was hired as a central office school administrator. During my interview for a teaching position in the district, the personnel officer encouraged me to take a position at Jefferson High School. She called Jefferson High an inner city high school whose quality was decreasing. I decided to take that position. When I entered school the first day that students attended, I was nervous. I am always nervous on the first day, but this was different. In some ways I was a little scared because in my limited experience as a teacher, I had never taught in a school labeled "inner city." As a result of my preconceived notions of inner city schools, I had visions of disruptive, unruly, and unmotivated students in the halls and in my classes.

The students I greeted at the door of my classroom were not disruptive or unruly. They were polite, very well dressed, and enthusiastic, and they seemed to be excited to be in my mathematics classes. I learned quickly that this school and its students were similar to the schools where I had previously taught—a normal school with a diverse student population. I was comfortable. But in every perfect situation, an enigma can arise.

My enigma the first few days of school was Alfred[1]. He was a rather large tenth-grade boy who was enrolled in Algebra Concepts 2—the second year of a two-year course in Algebra 1. Alfred looked like he played football, because he was about six-foot-two, muscular, and very well developed. In the first few days of class, it became apparent that Alfred was testing me and my ability to both control the class and teach algebra. Even though Alfred did not always have his homework ready for class, he did not refuse to do his work. His ability and motivation to complete class work were not the problem; it was his behavior. He was disruptive, sarcastic, and in some situations demeaning to other students. Considering this conduct, I was not sure of a strategy to use to diffuse his need to challenge both the other students and me and to help him become serious about learning algebra.

> **It became apparent that Alfred was testing me and my ability to both control the class and teach algebra.**

After thinking for several days, I decided that I would demonstrate through my behavior that Alfred was special to me. I decided to say something special to him every day as he entered the room. Because this scenario occurred at the beginning of the year, I knew nothing of Alfred's life or his aspirations. All I knew was that I wanted him to know that I welcomed him in my class and that I cared about more than just his knowledge and performance in mathematics. My question or comment to Alfred varied from day to day. Generally I asked him about the school and professional football games, how his previous weekend or evening was, his view on something that I had seen in the newspaper or on the television news, or whether he had difficulty with the homework assignment. I just wanted to engage him in a brief conversation.

After about two weeks of my talking with him before class, I was surprised that Alfred started to come to my class earlier and earlier. His behavior in class improved, and he actually started completing his homework assignments with some concern about how well he achieved. Certainly he was still playful in class, and we laughed a lot, but he no longer challenged me for the direction of class. More important was that Alfred began to learn algebra. He was motivated to do mathematics because he believed that he could be successful, and he knew that he would have my support when he had difficulty. With his new efforts I became aware that he was an average to above-average student in mathematics. Alfred became one of my successful students. He even requested to take geometry during the next school year.

> **Alfred was motivated to do mathematics because he believed that he could be successful.**

As fate would have it, I was scheduled to teach geometry that year and was to be Alfred's teacher. I was surprised when he told me later that he had made sure that he was signed up for my course. I had the privilege of teaching Alfred in three mathematics classes in three years. Certainly the years were not totally without challenges. I can remember many situations in which I had to pull him out the classroom for private conversations because of his interactions with other students. But Alfred received the conversations with respect and his understanding of my concern for his achievement and emotional development. The relationship that Alfred and I forged had transcended his constant need to disguise his lack of confidence by trying to exert power and control in class and had become

---

1. Name is a pseudonym.

one of mutual respect, reflecting his belief that he could be successful in mathematics. Alfred graduated from high school and was accepted into college. Our close relationship has lasted over the years and will last for our lifetime. This relationship and his understanding of mathematics were enhanced, in part, by my asking him one question a day to let him know that I cared about him and his learning.

The strategy used in this instance demonstrates the power of a teacher's care and concern for a student. Even though the vignette described is from a high school class, the strategy presented can be used at any grade level. Here is a quote from a sixteen-year-old student who remembered his third-grade teacher as a motivating factor in his life (Burke 1996, p. 21):

> My third-grade teacher was the best. She made sure I learned. She taught me right from wrong. And she kept me out of trouble. She told me to be a leader, not a follower. And that's what I've done. She gave me pride and self-confidence. She made me understand what life is all about and how important it is to plan your life. Today I believe in myself. I'm never going to let her down.

Similarly as in my relationship with Alfred, the third-grade teacher described seems to have demonstrated care and concern for her student that stayed with him throughout his schooling. Just as displaying care can encourage change in students' reaction to learning and views of themselves, appropriate classroom instructional strategies that focus on the specific needs of students can result in academic success in heterogeneous mathematics classrooms.

Focus of This Three-Book Series

As we strive to give students in classrooms from prekindergarten through grade twelve opportunities to experience and learn mathematics that will serve them throughout their lifetime, increasingly more teachers are presented with classrooms of students with a range of needs, backgrounds, expertise, and experience, including students who lack prerequisite skills and students who may be able to move forward quickly and with deep understanding. Recognizing that all classrooms are diverse, this NCTM series of three books (for grades Pre-K–5, 6–8, and 9–12) addresses instructional strategies that meet the needs of all students and offer them high-quality mathematics. The mathematical instructional strategies presented in these books reflect that diversity can come in the form of language, culture, race, gender, socioeconomic status, and ways of learning and thinking, as well as cognitive and emotional characteristics.

Guided by the vision of the NCTM *Principles and Standards* (2000) document, which states, "Equity ... demands that reasonable and appropriate accommodations be made as needed to promote access and attainment for all students" (p. 12), these books are designed to help teachers meet the diverse needs of their students. The volumes focus on helping teachers determine *how* to support high-quality mathematics learning for diverse

Instructional strategies that focus on the specific needs of students can result in academic success in heterogeneous mathematics classrooms.

Diversity can come in the form of language, culture, race, gender, socioeconomic status, and ways of learning and thinking, as well as cognitive and emotional characteristics.

student populations in a given classroom. The articles in this volume are presented in one of three forms: (1) cases of classroom practice, (2) instructional strategies, and (3) teacher development.

- Case articles describe classroom practice that promotes the learning of all students. They offer rich descriptions of teachers' practice, students' activity, and students' resulting learning.

- Instructional-strategies articles offer glimpses of the implementation or impact of particular instructional practices that support mathematical learning, not only for one group of students but for students having many diverse needs. These articles give examples of instruction or mathematical tasks that are beneficial for all students but especially relevant to students not well served by traditional approaches.

- Teacher-development articles discuss important topics to help teachers develop their expertise with teaching students who have a range of needs, backgrounds, and experience.

We are pleased to offer articles that span the issues and recommendations for our practice in the education of all students in mathematics.

In this grades 9–12 volume of the Mathematics for All Students series we are pleased to offer articles that span the issues and recommendations for our practice in the education of all students in mathematics. A brief description of each of the articles in this book follows.

Synopses of Articles

Fran Arbaugh and Patty Avery in article 1, "Enhancing the Learning Environment through Student Led Mathematical Discussions," show how teachers can create a learning environment that allows students to lead mathematical discussions. Such discussions involve many students, and the teacher helps students tie together mathematical concepts. The students in charge of the discussion prompt reflection, ask open-ended questions, and ask for explanations. Students also work in small groups in which they contribute to the small-group discussion and thinking. This practice is crucial for students who may have difficulty speaking in whole-group format.

In "Facilitating Whole-Class Discussion in Diverse Classrooms," article 2, Rebecca McGraw, David Romero, and Robert Krueger describe strategies for engaging all students in a diverse first-year algebra class in whole-class discussions in a lesson on linear functions. Teachers offer opportunities for students to develop ideas and opinions; uncover students' thinking; build discussion around students' solutions; encourage sharing, listening, and debate; make connections across representations; and introduce new problems and questions.

In article 3, "Mathematics Instruction and Academic English," Kerry Enright highlights the importance of language and describes ten strategies teachers can use to facilitate access to mathematics for second-language learners that can also help other students. Teachers use active voice at first; use simple verb tenses and constructions; use flow charts and graphic organizers; incorporate cognates; avoid introducing new ideas and new vocabulary together; simplify sentence structure; delay the use of pronouns;

repeat patterns of language and paraphrase; prioritize vocabulary; and make the language of mathematics more demanding over time.

In article 4, "Help One, Help All," Julie Sliva Spitzer, Dorothy White, and Alfinio Flores describe instructional strategies that are designed to address the needs of specific students but that actually support all students' learning of mathematics. The authors highlight such strategies as the use of multiple representations and making connections, as well as the importance of teachers' creating learning environments that engage and support all types of learners.

In "Yes, You Can," article 5, Sandie Gilliam, Jennifer Lahey, and Megan Staples describe how a high school mathematics teacher and a special education teacher combined their teaching to support students in a low-level mathematics course and in a special education course to give them access to algebra and allow them to be successful. They emphasized sense making with the Interactive Mathematics Program.

Janet St. Clair, Jamye Carter, and Sibyl St. Clair emphasize the importance of reading in mathematics in article 6, "Using a 'New Synthesis of Reading in Mathematics' to Encourage Disadvantaged High School Students to Be a Community of Mathematicians." Students read historical sketches and used such reading strategies as say something, cloning an author, and sketch-to-sketch.

José Contreras, in "Generating Problems, Conjectures, and Theorems with Interactive Geometry," article 7, uses Varignon's theorem in the context of an interactive geometry environment to describe prototypical problem-posing strategies. From a given problem students generate new problems, such as proof problems, special problems, general problems, and extended problems. At the end the author reflects on adapting and differentiating the investigation for diverse learners.

Armando Martínez-Cruz and José Contreras in article 8, "Egyptian Fractions, a Graphing Calculator, and Rational Functions," illustrate how such modern tools as graphing calculators can give all students access to mathematical ideas and help them make connections among several topics by using rational functions to express a fraction as the sum of unit fractions.

Mark Ellis in article 9, "Moving from Deficiencies to Possibilities," offers theoretical insights about differentiation by varying instruction to furnish greater access and learning opportunities for all, in contrast with by giving some students fewer opportunities and less access on the basis of perceived deficits. In addition he gives examples of how preconceptions about students can be very limiting for their learning, and examples of how teachers who expect students to learn and offer different ways to access mathematics can make a difference in terms of students' performance in mathematics.

In article 10, "Why Discourse Deserves Our Attention!" Beth Herbel-Eisenmann, Michelle Cirillo, and Kathryn Skowronksi explain why teachers of mathematics need to pay conscious attention to classroom discourse. The four reasons they address are that (1) mathematics is a specialized form of literacy, (2) spoken language is a primary mode of teaching and learning, (3) the particular context in which language is used plays a role in what is appropriate to say and do, and (4) language is intimately related to culture and identity. They also illustrate how teachers can improve classroom discourse practices through reading groups and action research.

George Bright and Jeane Joyner in article 11, "Discussions of Mathematical Thinking," show how discussions play a crucial role in formative assessment and present ways in which teachers can be more effective in reaching all students by becoming better at leading discussions. Some of the ways are asking an engaging question to begin, deciding which student should respond, listening carefully to a student's response, making inferences about what knowledge is revealed, asking follow-up questions to probe thinking, paraphrasing a student's response, and summarizing the discussion. The decisions that teachers need to make as they guide a discussion are also analyzed.

In article 12, "Learning from One Another," Fran Arbaugh describes a model of professional development based on an observation-and-debriefing cycle with colleagues. The observed teacher tells the observers what she would like to be the focus of the observation. They observe one class period and take field notes, followed by a one-hour debriefing. All write about what they learned as observers or observed. Arbaugh also gives six practical guidelines to create a study group with your colleagues.

—Carol E. Malloy
Series Editor

REFERENCES

Burke, Nancy. *Teachers Are Special.* New York: Random House, 1996.

Marquis, David M., and Robin Sachs. *I Am a Teacher: A Tribute to America's Teachers.* New York: Simon & Schuster, 1990.

McLeod, Douglas B. "Research on Learning and Instruction in Mathematics: The Role of Affect." In *Integrating Research on Teaching and Learning Mathematics: Papers from the First Wisconsin Symposium for Research on Teaching and Learning Mathematics,* edited by Elizabeth Fennema, Thomas P. Carpenter, and Susan J. Lamon, pp. 55–82. Albany: State University of New York, 1991.

National Council of Teachers of Mathematics (NCTM). *Principles and Standards for School Mathematics.* Reston, Va.: NCTM, 2000.

Enhancing the Learning Environment through Student-Led Mathematical Discussions

Fran Arbaugh
Patricia L. Avery

Teachers establish and nurture an environment conducive to learning mathematics through the decisions they make, the conversations they orchestrate, and the physical setting they create. Teachers' actions are what encourage students to think, question, solve problems, and discuss their ideas, strategies, and solutions. The teacher is responsible for creating an intellectual environment where serious mathematical thinking is the norm. More than just a physical setting with desks, bulletin boards, and posters, the classroom environment communicates subtle messages about what is valued in learning and doing mathematics. Are students' discussion and collaboration encouraged? Are students expected to justify their thinking? If students are to learn to make conjectures, experiment with various approaches to solving problems, construct mathematical arguments and respond to others' arguments, then creating an environment that fosters these kinds of activities is essential.

—*National Council of Teachers of Mathematics*

THIS passage from *Principles and Standards for School Mathematics* (NCTM 2000, p. 18) suggests a mathematics classroom in which the teacher creates opportunities for students to talk about mathematics in a meaningful way. The authors of *Principles and Standards* argue that this type of classroom supports *all students* in learning meaningful mathematics. However, as many teachers know, achieving this kind of environment is often a challenging endeavor. When working with high school mathematics teachers during professional development, we often hear such comments as, "I know that I am supposed to be creating a supportive environment for my students, but I'm just not sure what to do differently."

In this article, we describe a facet of Patty's (coauthor and high school mathematics teacher) classroom practice that fosters students' discourse. We first set the stage with a short description of Patty's school and classroom. We then present an episode from Patty's classroom during which her high school mathematics students take charge of orchestrating whole-class discussion around a mathematical task.

Patty's Classroom

Patty is a high school mathematics teacher for Columbia (Missouri) Public Schools, a district that has approximately 16,000 students in grades K–12. Rock Bridge High School, where Patty is on faculty, has approximately 1,800 students in grades 10–12. Patty is a veteran teacher, having taught mathematics in grades 7–12 for more than thirty years. Patty has been active in many professional development activities throughout her teaching career, most recently as a participant in a professional development project directed by Fran Arbaugh (the other coauthor).

The classroom episode described in this article took place in Patty's high school mathematics class in which the students' textbook is *Contemporary Mathematics in Context,* part of the Core-Plus curriculum. The students enrolled in this Course 3 class were mostly sophomores. Prior to this classroom episode, students had been working in small groups on the task presented in figure 1.1.

The following table shows the average monthly Fahrenheit temperatures for Des Moines, Iowa.

Month	Jan	Feb	Mar	Apr	May	June	July	Aug	Sept	Oct	Nov	Dec
Temperature	19	25	37	51	62	72	77	74	65	54	39	24

a. Plot the (month, temperature) data using 0 for January, 1 for February, and so on. On the same plot, sketch a graph that fits the data.

b. What function family best fits the data?

c. What is the amplitude of the modeling function?

d. What is the period of the modeling function?

e. Do the data indicate a horizontal shift from the basic toolkit function for this function's family? Do the data indicate a vertical shift?

f. Write a symbolic rule that gives average monthly temperature as a function of the month.

g. Compare your function rule with the rules of other groups. Resolve any differences.

h. Use your function model to estimate the average monthly temperature for the month of April. Compare the temperature as reported in the table with your estimate.

Fig. 1.1 Temperatures task used as basis for student-led discussion

Adapted from *Contemporary Mathematics in Context,* Course 3, Part B (Coxford et al. 2003, p. 467). Used with permission of Glencoe/McGraw Hill.

Over the past few years, Patty has been striving to find ways to encourage students' greater involvement in whole-class discussions. She said,

> After much exploration, study, and collaboration with others, I finally decided to make a commitment to cultivate more student-centered mathematical authority in my classroom and to hold myself as well as my students accountable for the success of this change. I knew I had to say less and allow my students to process the concepts. I wanted them to think mathematically, not just complete procedures by rote. This meant providing more time for them to collaborate in small groups and allowing them the authority and opportunity to lead whole-class discussions with less input from me. Only by turning over to them the entire experience of learning, would they learn how to learn.

On the basis of her motivation to strive to include all students in her classroom, Patty developed an environment in which her students took responsibility for leading whole-class discussions. In the next section, we describe an episode from Patty's classroom.

A Peek inside Patty's Classroom

On the day of this episode, Katie and Susan volunteered to lead the discussion for the problem shown in figure 1.1. As they moved to the front of the room, Patty found a place in the back of the room from which to observe and contribute to the subsequent conversation. In the following piece of classroom transcript,[1] we visited Patty's classroom during the student-led discussion about parts b, c, d, and e of the problem. Katie enters data on the overhead graphing calculator and sets the dimensions for the graph to be displayed.

Susan (L):	What function family best fits the data?
Ashley:	It's a periodic function.
Susan (L):	Good job! Does everybody agree it's a periodic function? What kind?
Ashley:	Sine.
Patty (T):	What do you guys think about that so far? It's a periodic function, and it'll be sine?
Zack:	It could be cosine.
Patty (T):	Oh! It could be cosine? *(Some chatter ripples around the room discussing this.)* Sometimes one will lend itself to an easier match than the other. I'm hearing that we've got votes for sine and cosine. Ladies, part c?

---

1. In this transcript, discussion leaders are designated with "L" and Patty (the teacher), with "T."

After much exploration, study, and collaboration with others, I finally decided to make a commitment to cultivate more student-centered mathematical authority in my classroom and to hold myself as well as my students accountable for the success of this change.

Susan (L):	What is the amplitude of the modeling function, and how did you find that? [The question actually reads: What is the amplitude of the modeling function? Susan took the opportunity here to extend the question from part c.]
Lauren:	The amplitude equals 29, and I found it because I took the highest point, which is 77, minus the lowest point, which is 19, and I divided it by 2 and that equals 29.
Susan (L):	OK! Good job! What about the period? [Susan is asking about part d: What is the period of the modeling function?] Scott?
Scott:	4π.
Katie (L):	How'd you do that?
Scott:	Uh, k equals 2π, and I divided that by 0.5
Page:	Wouldn't you divide by 2?
Katie (L):	That would be for finding the amplitude.
Page:	Oh, right. I got it.

This exchange was followed by small-group discussion of period, with students seeking to make sense of the difference between amplitude and period. As discussion slows, Katie went back to Scott's answer of dividing by 0.5.

Katie (L):	Scott, can you tell us where you got the 0.5 you used to divide?
Mark:	[Mark is Scott's partner] I think we took that 0.47 and kinda rounded up. And well, yeah, we didn't know.
Katie (L):	Does anyone know where the 0.5 came from?

At this point, Patty realized that instead of analyzing the graph, Scott and Mark used the regression feature of their graphing calculator to find the amplitude and period, reading from the regression equation.

Patty (T):	We're going to back off from the regression equation for the time being. We'll use it as a check later on.

During small-group work on this problem, Patty noticed that the members of Allison's group realized how to find the period from reading the graph.

Patty (T):	Allison, I am going to call on you, because when we asked a minute ago about the period, you had a big, sheepish grin on your face.
Allison:	It's kind of embarrassing, because I was making it harder than it was. Because you are doing average temperature, and Sneha pointed out that it was twelve months. So that would be the amplitude.
Patty (T):	Careful!
Allison:	Oh, sorry. Period.
[*Some small group discussion follows this exchange.*]	
Susan (L):	[*Reading part e of the problem*] Do the data indicate a horizontal shift from the basic toolkit function for this function's family? Do the data indicate a vertical shift?
Zack:	I said "no" for horizontal and "yes" for vertical.
Matt:	It could be both.
Patty (T):	You say it could be both?
Matt:	If you use the sine, there is horizontal shift.
Patty (T):	That was "if"? You said "if" to qualify your answer? What if it is not sine?
Matt:	Then it's only a vertical shift.
Patty (T):	What do you all think about a vertical shift?

At this point, Katie took over as discussion leader, and referred to the graph showing on the overhead graphing calculator screen as she explained.

Katie (L):	If you look at the graph, you see that this is your y-axis, this is your x-axis, [and] this is your origin. So if you look at it, no matter what you do, you will see that there is always a horizontal shift because even if this was cosine, it would still be a horizontal shift because the peak would be over there [*pointing to the y-intercept of y = cosine(x)*].
Lindsay:	What?

Katie removed the graphing calculator projection unit from the overhead and sketched a coordinate plane. On that graph, she sketched the function from this problem.

11

Katie (L):	Like, OK. This is (0, 0). If you move up, then this is the *y*-intercept of the regular cosine graph. So our graph is shifting.
David:	It could be the opposite of a cosine function.
Patty (T):	You bet. It could be the opposite. I heard Angela saying that, too.
Angela:	It could be a reflection.
Patty (T):	Are you getting the feeling that either answer you give, you could make it work for sine or cosine?
Class:	[*Murmurs around the room – "yes."*]
Patty (T):	What about the second part of question e?
Susan (L):	If we're using sine, we've already said that there's vertical shift. There is vertical shift; well, you could do either sine or cosine.
Hayden:	There is vertical shift.
Katie (L):	Why is there vertical shift?
Hayden:	Well, for basic sine, the midline would be at zero.
Patty (T):	Where is our midline?

The environment that Patty established in her classroom encouraged engagement by all students, making it safe to contribute in front of peers.

At this point, Patty sensed that many students needed help in thinking about the vertical shift. She moved on to a short discussion of part e, using one group's incomplete work on part e to stimulate discussion about vertical shift. Patty asked many questions during this time, prompting students to make connections among what they knew about amplitude, vertical shift, and midline.

Several interesting things happen in this episode, a few of which we note below:

- This discussion involved many students. The environment that Patty established in her classroom encouraged engagement by all students, making it safe to contribute in front of peers.

- Patty did not fade into the background completely during this discussion. Her role as teacher was especially important in helping her students connect important mathematical concepts.

- Katie and Susan took back the lead in the discussion with no prompting from Patty.

- Katie and Susan did not engage in "show and tell." They prompted reflection, asked open-ended questions, and asked for explanations.

The roles that the student leaders and Patty played in this classroom are different from teacher and student roles typically found in U. S. mathematics classrooms. Patty, as the teacher, expected Katie and Susan to facilitate discussion, not tell their peers how to solve the problem, and Katie and Susan met that expectation.

The roles that the student leaders and Patty played in this classroom are different from teacher and student roles typically found in U. S. mathematics classrooms. Patty, as the teacher, expected Katie and Susan to facilitate discussion, not tell their peers how to solve the problem, and Katie and

Susan met that expectation. In turn, Patty had to yield total authority in the classroom, trusting that her student leaders would facilitate competently.

Incorporating Student-Led Discussions into Your Instruction

If you decide to incorporate student-led discussions in your classroom, an important point to keep in mind is that Patty's and her students' practice did not develop overnight. Patty has worked hard at learning new instructional strategies that improve her classroom environment. In turn, her students have responded to Patty's efforts with cooperation and enthusiasm. "How," you might be wondering, "does Patty get her students to do this?" Patty articulates that process below, and then offers advice for teachers who want to incorporate student-led discussion into their instruction.

Patty starts by explaining how she begins the school year with a new group of students:

> In the beginning, this process of change involves me modeling the process of leading discussions. In the first weeks of a new school year, I invite a small group to the front of the room to lead along side of me. I hand over the marker to one of my students to record all thoughts suggested from the class, promising the volunteer group and the class that being in the front of the class is the safest place to be. I tell them, "You only write down what others tell you." Then I begin modeling how to ask questions. I have one of the student leaders read the problem. (Remember, the class members have already had the opportunity to work on the assigned problem in their small groups.) I then ask the class where they started with the information and what they did to solve it. Over the course of the next couple of weeks, I begin to move away from the front of the room when students are leading discussions, removing myself from the focal point of the class. I direct less and less each class period. My contributions to the conversations from then on are more questioning and encouraging, specifically highlighting what the students have done well—pointing out that they do not need my input, that they have all they need to solve the problems.

A straight path does not exist to the point where your students engage in the types of discussion described previously in this article. Some days your students will do well with this organization; other days they may be a bit contentious about the whole idea. Be patient! Remember that your goal is to include more and more students in whole-class discussions, and that change—for you and your students—takes time.

On the basis of her experiences, Patty has some encouraging words of advice for teachers who try this strategy in their classrooms:

- Just try it! Start by choosing a problem for which the answer is not readily evident, that requires some problem-solving strategies and is not simply procedural. Have students work in small groups on the

Remember that your goal is to include more and more students in whole-class discussions, and that change— for you and your students—takes time.

problem, and then invite a group to the front to lead the discussion as described in the foregoing.

- You might have to change your mindset and let go of expectations that hold you back. For example, I had to let go of my desire for total control over the pace and direction of discussion. As I let go, I realized that my students sometimes took us to places mathematically that we would not have gone had I maintained total control.

- This type of student-centered learning is messy and slow. When students explore a situation, really grappling with the mathematics, you may find that the pace of the class slows. I have learned to do the same work we did before, but in a different fashion.

- Be patient, and keep trying. Have patience with yourself and with your students. This process will always be a work-in-progress, at times messy, time-consuming, and noisy.

- Develop high expectations for students. They can assume more responsibility for their own learning, be actively involved, learn to collaborate with others in small and large groups, and lead large-group discussions.

- Welcome wrong ideas and answers—making errors is not failing; those errors create a great opportunity during a lesson. If the leaders make a mistake, their classmates will usually notice; allow students to find the leaders' error and suggest corrections.

As Patty incorporated more student-led discussions into her mathematics classroom, she noted changes in her students over the years. The following statements reflect the positive outcomes you may see from your students.

- Students learn to lead large-class discussion by asking questions, not by doing a "show and tell" act.

- Students learn leadership skills. They learn to think on their feet, improve their public-speaking skills and their interpersonal skills, display a certain amount of courage, develop confidence in their preparation for leading, learn how to prepare, and develop empathy for the mathematical struggles of their classmates.

- Overall, students in a class with this type of environment learn to be self-reliant and to collaborate in small groups. They learn to articulate and justify their own thoughts, listen to others, communicate and reflect on their thinking orally and in writing, read technical material, articulate their own questions, and be advocates for their own learning.

When students lead class discussions, they justify their own thinking, examine the ideas of others very carefully, and become critical friends to one another. They learn to rely on themselves as the mathematical authority.

Having students lead whole-group discussion is just one of the ways that Patty seeks to include all learners in engaging in mathematics during class. One other strategy Patty uses is to have students work in small groups regularly, encouraging all members of each group to contribute to

Develop high expectations for students. They can assume more responsibility for their own learning, be actively involved, learn to collaborate with others in small and large groups, and lead large-group discussions.

When students lead class discussions, they justify their own thinking, examine the ideas of others very carefully, and become critical friends to one another. They learn to rely on themselves as the mathematical authority.

the small-group discussion and thinking. Patty believes that this practice opens up space for students who might be shy when speaking in a whole-group format. For example, Patty remembers a student named Madison, whose first language was Spanish. At the time that Madison was in Patty's class, she had lived in United States for two years and was continuing to develop fluency in English. Madison was shy and reserved in the class. Patty observed that, during whole-class discussions, Madison was most often an observer. "However," Patty says,

> I noticed Madison being much more open and involved in her small group than when we worked as a large group. At times after students had had time to process with their group partners, I even noticed her speaking out in large-class discussion with confidence. She had already had the chance to process her thinking with her group and to share her ideas and receive feedback from her partners. This small-group time gave Madison the opportunity to see how the language was used and to adapt it to her own thinking. She was a sponge with her partners, and this type of collaborative learning strengthened her language skills as she became accustomed to the language usage.

Patty believes that small-group work is supportive not just of English language learners but of any student who may have difficulty talking out in large-group discussion. An example is Kayle, a student who had serious brain surgery a few years before she was in Patty's class. Patty describes Kayle as "a bright student, but one who felt an extreme amount of stress when in the spotlight." Because of this feeling of stress, Kayle would not come to the front of the room to lead discussions. However, as Patty describes,

> Kayle was very comfortable in her "home group" and was a strong and very trusted contributor to their work. At times during whole-class discussion, I would hear Kayle make a quiet comment, sharing insight or an answer. When this happened, I would highlight her good ideas in the whole-class discussion. For Kayle, having the familiar group of buddies to try out her own thoughts was a good starting point.

Patty finds this tendency to be true of all her students, most of whom need to build their mathematical confidence with the support of others.

Small-group work is supportive not just of English language learners but of any student who may have difficulty talking out in large-group discussion.

Conclusion

Professional Standards for Teaching Mathematics (NCTM 1991) contains recommendations for teachers and students with regard to classroom discourse (p. 45):

> The teacher of mathematics should promote classroom discourse in which students —

- listen to, respond to, and question the teacher and one another;

- use a variety of tools to reason, make connections, solve problems, and communicate;

- initiate problems and questions;

- make conjectures and present solutions;

- explore examples and counterexamples to investigate a conjecture;

- try to convince themselves and one another of the validity of particular representations, solutions, conjectures, and answers;

- rely on mathematical evidence and argument to determine validity.

Incorporating student-led discussions into your mathematics instruction can be an effective instructional strategy for realizing this type of environment—one in which *every student* has the opportunity to contribute and learn.

REFERENCES

Coxford, Arthur F., et al. *Contemporary Mathematics in Context: A Unified Approach.* Course 3, Part B. New York: Glencoe McGraw-Hill, 2003.

National Council of Teachers of Mathematics (NCTM). *Professional Standards for Teaching Mathematics.* Reston, Va.: NCTM, 1991.

———. *Principles and Standards for School Mathematics.* Reston, Va.: NCTM, 2000.

2

Facilitating Whole-Class Discussions in Diverse Classrooms: Strategies for Engaging All Students

Rebecca McGraw
David Romero
Robert Krueger

ENGAGING diverse groups of students in discussions about mathematics is important because students' strategies often vary and "thinking about multiple solutions can promote deeper thinking about mathematics" (Burrill 1998, p. 189). When students are allowed to develop solutions that make sense to them, group work can furnish a basis for explorations of various solutions and solution methods during whole-class discussions. In this article, we describe a lesson on linear functions that we used with a diverse group of first-year-algebra students, including strategies for engaging all students in whole-class discussions. Although described in the context of a secondary school lesson, the strategies could be used with elementary school students as well. Readers who would like addition information about the lesson on linear functions should see McGraw, Romero, and Krueger (2006). The six sections of this article correspond to six strategies for building and facilitating mathematics discussions: (1) providing opportunities for students to develop ideas and opinions; (2) uncovering students' thinking; (3) building discussion around students' solutions; (4) encouraging sharing, listening, and debate; (5) making connections across representations; and (6) inserting new problems and questions.

Providing Opportunities for Students to Develop Ideas and Opinions

Students are more willing to speak, and more likely to speak thoughtfully, when they have opportunities to reflect on and develop their ideas prior to whole-class discussion. Working in small groups on a common problem, students can communicate their thinking, discuss strategies, and develop opinions. Diversity within and across groups leads to variations in ideas and opinions—this diversity enriches both small-group and whole-class discussion.

In the Stadium Seating problem, students investigate the height above the ground of a set of stadium bleachers. Before going outside to collect

Students are more willing to speak, and more likely to speak thoughtfully, when they have opportunities to reflect on and develop their ideas prior to whole-class discussion.

data, students are shown a sketch of the stadium bleachers and asked three questions (see fig. 2.1).

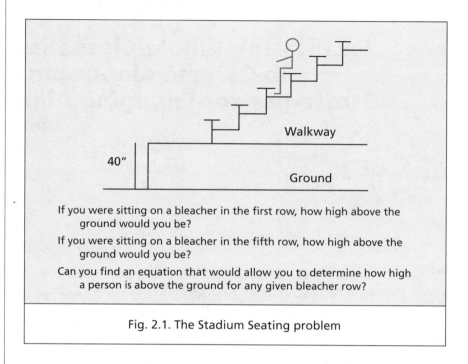

If you were sitting on a bleacher in the first row, how high above the ground would you be?

If you were sitting on a bleacher in the fifth row, how high above the ground would you be?

Can you find an equation that would allow you to determine how high a person is above the ground for any given bleacher row?

Fig. 2.1. The Stadium Seating problem

Working in small groups, the students decide what data they will need to collect to answer the questions. Outside, they use tape measures or measuring sticks to collect real data from their school's football (or basketball) stadium and then represent their data in tables, graphs, equations, and words (see fig. 2.2). The investigation brings forth students' understandings—and misunderstandings—about linear relationships and their representations. The work students produce is then collected by the teacher and becomes fodder for the following day's whole-class discussion.

Uncovering Students' Thinking

Examples of stadium measurements and student work are shown in figures 2.3 and 2.4.

Beginning algebra students' ability to graph the bleacher data and find equations that accurately represent the relationship between bleacher number and bleacher height varies greatly. For example, David and Melinda were able to measure the distance between the walkway and the first bleacher (17 inches) and the height of the first bleacher (57 inches). Melinda correctly found the change in bleacher height to be 10 inches per bleacher, whereas David appeared to believe that each subsequent seat will be 17 inches higher above the ground than the previous seat. Conversely, David was able to graph the data accurately from his table, whereas Melinda incorrectly numbered her y-axis and did not use evenly spaced intervals.

Both Seth and Rosario were able to represent the bleacher-height-to-number relationship algebraically. Seth used 57 inches as a constant and

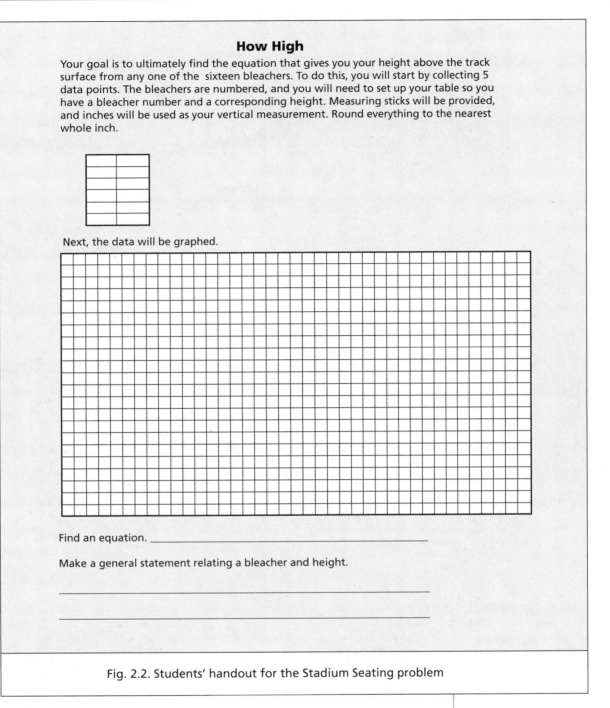

How High

Your goal is to ultimately find the equation that gives you your height above the track surface from any one of the sixteen bleachers. To do this, you will start by collecting 5 data points. The bleachers are numbered, and you will need to set up your table so you have a bleacher number and a corresponding height. Measuring sticks will be provided, and inches will be used as your vertical measurement. Round everything to the nearest whole inch.

Next, the data will be graphed.

Find an equation. _____

Make a general statement relating a bleacher and height.

_____

_____

Fig. 2.2. Students' handout for the Stadium Seating problem

multiplied by $x - 1$ rather than by x, because the 10-inch-per-bleacher rate did not hold for the first bleacher. Rosario used 17 as the rate of change but subtracted 7 from all but the first bleacher to adjust for the difference between the first bleacher and the rest of the bleachers. Rosario's table, graph, and equation match, but Seth's table and graph do not match his algebraic expression. All but one point in the table and graph match the function $57 + 10x = y$. Looking across solutions, we can see that only one student numbered the y-axis consistently beginning with zero, three students wrote equations, and one student drew a line through the points on the graph.

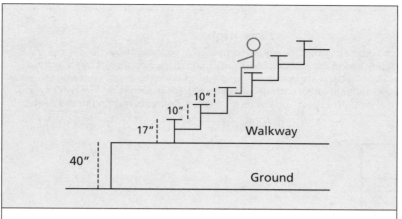

Fig. 2.3. Diagram of football stadium bleachers with measurements

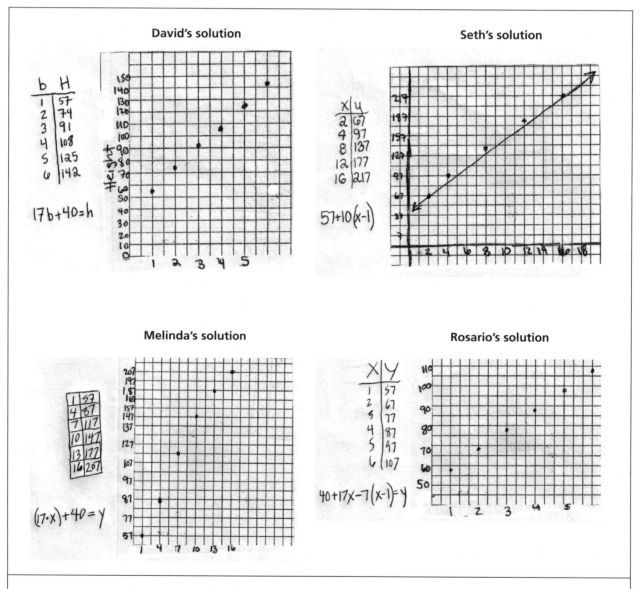

Fig. 2.4. Examples of students' solutions to the Stadium Seating problem

Because students were allowed to make decisions about table values, graph scales, and equation forms, students' thinking became more visible to themselves and to us. Understanding how students think can help teachers facilitate discussion in ways that support the learning of all students—including those who would generally choose not to speak during whole-class discussions.

Building Discussion around Students' Solutions

An analysis of students' solutions can guide decisions about how best to begin whole-class discussions. With respect to the Stadium Seating problem, one method could be to select some of the students' algebraic representations (equations or expressions), write them across the top of the white board, and ask students how they found their equations. An example of this method is shown in Classroom Vignette 1.

Classroom Vignette 1

1. $47 + 10x = y$

2. $57 + 10x = y$

3. $(17x) + 10 = y$

4. $40 + 17b = h$

Mr. Ruiz:	I'm not worried about if an equation is right or wrong right now. I want to know how you got the numbers.
Jessie:	Well, for the first equation, if it's the first bleacher, then it has to be 57 above the ground because you add 40 plus 17, and the equation matches because it would be 47 plus 10.
	[*Mr. Ruiz creates a table showing "seat" and "height" as column headings beside the first equation. Mr. Ruiz writes "1" under "seat" and "57" under "height."*]
Mr. Ruiz:	Do you agree with Jessie that if we put 1 into the equation for *x*, then we will get 57 as our answer? [*Most students murmur "yes" as Mr. Ruiz writes 47 + 10(1) = y, 47 + 10 = y, and 57 = y underneath the first equation.*]
Mr. Ruiz:	What about seat 2? [*Mr. Ruiz enters 2 into the table and leads the class in substituting 2 into the equation to get 67.*] So, is 67 what we should get?
Marisa:	Yes, because you just do 10 times 2 plus 47.
Mr. Ruiz:	Yes, you are right, that's what the equation

21

	gives us. But do 57 and 67 make sense in terms of the stadium seats? [*Mr. Ruiz moves so that he is standing next to the diagram on the white board of the stadium seats.*]
Marisa:	First you add 17, but after that you add 10, so it has to go up by 10 each time.
Javier:	Yeah. It has to be 77, 87, 97. It just keeps going.
Mr. Ruiz:	[*to the class*] What measurements did you come up with when you were outside? How high was the first seat above the walkway? Marisa says first she added 17. [*to Marisa*] Do you mean 17 inches from the walkway to the first seat? [*Marisa nods*] What did other people find?
Jeff:	Our group got 17 for each seat. When you go from one seat to the next, I mean, we got 17 each time. We got $40 + 17b$.
Marisa:	But it is only 17 the first time. It's less for the rest because the seats stick up.
	[*At this point, Mr. Ruiz uses the diagram of the stadium seats to aid students in analyzing the difference between repeatedly adding 17 and repeatedly adding 10. Consensus develops among the students that the vertical distance between seats is 10 inches, not 17, and Mr. Ruiz adds these measurements to the diagram (see fig. 2.2).*]
Mr. Ruiz:	So we can fill in the table for the first equation now, right? If we keep adding 10, we'll get 77, then 87, then 97 for seats 3, 4, and 5. Does that match our diagram? [Students nod.] OK.

Mr. Ruiz begins by asking students "how they got their numbers," which puts students' ways of thinking at the center of the discussion. After ensuring that the class understands that substituting 1 and 2 into the equation will result in 57 and 67, respectively, Mr. Ruiz asks, "Is 67 what we should get?" and "do 57 and 67 make sense?" These questions turn students' attention to the stadium seats themselves. The diagram of the stadium seats is meaningful to students in part because they can connect it with their experience measuring the heights themselves.

Having analyzed his students' work from the previous day, Mr. Ruiz knows that some students did not notice, or at least did not account for, the change in the rate of change between the first bleacher (17 inches) and the remaining bleachers (10 inches). Therefore, he focuses discussion quickly on this aspect of the problem. As discussion facilitator, Mr. Ruiz's goal is to move the discussion in a mathematically productive direction and at the same time ensure that the mathematics builds out of, and is connected with, students' ways of thinking.

Encouraging Sharing, Listening, and Debate

As the discussion moves forward, Mr. Ruiz continues to connect the numbers in the tables and equations with students' experiences measuring the bleacher heights. At the same time, he encourages students to share varying solutions and methods, as well as to assess one another's thinking with such questions as "Do you agree with Jessie …?" "So, is 67 what we should get?" and "What did other people find?" When students' ideas contradict one another—for example, when Marisa and Jeff disagree about whether to add 10 or 17—Mr. Ruiz engages students in analyzing the diagram of the stadium seats and using appropriate mathematical reasoning to determine which solution is correct.

The methods Mr. Ruiz modeled for analyzing the first equation are used again by the class as they analyze the second equation.

Classroom Vignette 2

Mr. Ruiz:	How about the second equation? [$57 + 10x = y$]
Nick:	Well, the equation's not right.
Mr. Ruiz:	How do you know?
Nick:	The numbers will be off.
Mr. Ruiz:	The numbers in the table? What will those numbers be?
Nick:	Well, for the first bleacher you'd have 67.
	[*As Nick speaks, Mr. Ruiz begins to draw a table underneath the second equation. He enters 1 and 67 as the first values.*]
Mr. Ruiz:	[*to the class*] Is that what the equation gives? Viviana, what will the height be for seat 2 for this equation?
Viviana:	Umm, 77?
Mr. Ruiz:	How did you get that?
Viviana:	Well, 20 plus 57.
Mr. Ruiz:	OK. And the next seat?
Viviana:	Eighty-seven, then 97. Ten each time, like the other one. [*Mr. Ruiz continues to fill in the table according to Viviana's directions.*]
Nick:	But the numbers are still wrong—like they're ten too much each time.
Mr. Ruiz:	So we need to have ten less for each row in

	our table. How could we change the equation just slightly so that we would get ten less each time?
Javier:	You could just change the 57 to 47, then it would be the same as the first one.
Mr. Ruiz:	Yes, that would work. That would be a good idea. [*pause*] Does anyone see another way? [*long pause*] How about this? [*Mr. Ruiz writes 57 +10(x − 1) = y above the table and underneath the second equation. Then he makes a third column in the table.*]
Mr. Ruiz:	Try to find the heights using this equation. Does this equation work? [*Students do the calculations and agree that the equation works.*]
Mr. Ruiz:	Didn't I see this equation on the papers of one group? Who was that? [*Seth's group raises their hands.*] Did your table match this table?
Seth:	Well, for seat 2 we got 67, but for seat 4 we got 97. That's not right.
Mr. Ruiz:	Why do you say it isn't right?
Anna:	It should be 87, not 97. You can tell by looking at the seats, it's 57 plus two 10s, not three.
Seth:	Our graph is wrong, too.
Mr. Ruiz:	That's OK. Do you understand it now? OK.

Mr. Ruiz begins this part of the discussion by turning students' attention to the second equation. He supports Nick in explaining his thinking to the class by creating a table showing how "the numbers will be off"—that is, the numbers in the table will not match those produced by the first equation. By asking the class, "Is that what the equation gives?" Mr. Ruiz encourages students to decide whether they agree with Nick. Next, Mr. Ruiz raises the question of whether the equation could be altered to produce the correct bleacher heights, and then deliberately alters the equation in such a way as to produce the equation of Seth's group. Bringing Seth's group's equation into the discussion serves several purposes: first, the class has the opportunity to analyze a somewhat different looking, but equivalent, equation; second, the students in Seth's group have the opportunity to reflect on their own solution, including their table and graph; third, all students have the opportunity to review substitution and the order of operations as they test whether the equation generates the correct bleacher heights.

Making Connections across Representations

As they work through the Stadium Seating problem, students represent the linear function in multiple ways, including tables, pictures, graphs, equations, and words. Students' ability to construct and use these representations can vary greatly, and they often do not see how closely one representation is connected with another. When students share their thinking and analyze one another's tables, graphs, and equations, they further their understanding of these connections. They also develop important mathematical habits, including communicating ideas verbally, reasoning about mathematical relationships, and providing justification for solutions and methods. By moving back and forth across representations during whole-class discussion, Mr. Ruiz creates opportunities for students to make connections between representations that they know well and those that they are less comfortable with. For example, he assists students in using an equation to create a table and then compares values in the table with a diagram of the stadium seats. Later, students begin to compare tables with tables and equations with equations, and use their comparisons to justify whether the equations accurately represent the bleacher heights.

Students' ways of thinking are represented in the equations and expressions they write. For example, Rosario wrote $40 + 17x - 7(x - 1) = y$, and explained her equation as follows: "I took the walkway height and added $17x$ because that was the height for the first bleacher, but that was too much for each of the other bleachers, so I had to take seven away for each bleacher after the first one." By sharing thinking with classmates, students learn that seemingly different equations can represent the same relationship. Testing the equations by substituting numbers can provide additional evidence. After students have developed a sense of which equations are equivalent and why, teachers can demonstrate that each equation simplifies to $47 + 10x = y$.

Inserting New Problems and Questions

In a class of twenty-five or thirty students, it is unlikely that everyone will have a chance to speak during a single discussion. Further, students vary in their willingness to speak in front of their peers. One method for ensuring that all students remain intellectually engaged during discussion is to insert new problems and questions periodically. Mr. Ruiz uses this strategy as a way to engage all students in analyzing the third and fourth equations.

Classroom Vignette 3

Mr. Ruiz: Now, equations number 3 and 4 [$(17x) + 10 = y$ and $40 + 17b = h$] look different from the first two equations. Please take a couple of minutes and use these equations to find the heights for seats 1, 2, 3, and 4. Go ahead and do this whether or not one of these is your group's equation.

[Students construct tables while Mr. Ruiz moves among students and checks for understanding. At this point, the groups who wrote

> **Students' ability to construct and use these representations can vary greatly, and they often do not see how closely one representation is connected with another. When students share their thinking and analyze one another's tables, graphs, and equations, they further their understanding of these connections.**

> **One method for ensuring that all students remain intellectually engaged during discussion is to insert new problems and questions periodically.**

these equations realize that their equations do not correctly represent the heights of seats 1–4. Mr. Ruiz then puts the tables and values for equations 3 and 4 on the white board.]

Mr. Ruiz: OK. When we were outside, you had to collect data and then find an equation to represent the data. I'm going to ask you to do the opposite now. You have two equations, $(17x) + 10 = y$ and $40 + 17b = h$, and you have tables of values that go with those equations. Your job is to work with your group and draw a series of stadium seats for which $(17x) + 10 = y$ would be the correct equation. Of course the measurements for the heights will be different, but you can use the equation and table to figure out what those measurements would be. Once you have a diagram, I will check it, and then you can move on and do $40 + 17b = h$. Any questions?

Mr. Ruiz begins by asking the students to create the tables for equations 3 and 4. Next, instead of repeating the process of comparing the tables with the diagram of the stadium seats as a whole class, Mr. Ruiz creates a slightly different task—drawing diagrams for which the tables of values will be correct. By assigning the task to small groups, Mr. Ruiz has an opportunity to listen to the thinking of a wide variety of students and to once again build discussion firmly on students' ways of thinking.

Conclusion

The Stadium Seating problem gives students multiple opportunities to develop understanding of linear functions and make connections across representations. Throughout the lesson, students use symbols meaningfully, model a real-world relationship with mathematics, and improve their ability to create tables, graphs, and equations. Important connections can be made from students' work on the Stadium Seating problem with such concepts as rate of change and y-intercept.

Investigating students' thinking and building instruction based on students' understandings is crucial when working with diverse groups of students. Such problems as the Stadium Seating problem are as useful in this respect because they provide us with many opportunities to gain insight into how our students think about mathematics. The variations we find in students' methods of solution and levels of understanding become a resource on which we can draw during whole-class discussions. Once students become accustomed to listening to and analyzing one another's ways of thinking, they too begin to see how useful other students' ideas can be in their own learning of mathematics.

REFERENCES

Burrill, Gail. "Changes in Your Classrooms: From the Past to the Present to the Future." *Mathematics Teaching in the Middle School* 4 (November–December 1998): 184–90.

McGraw, Rebecca, David Romero, and Robert Krueger."How Far Up Am I? The Mathematics of Stadium Seating." *Mathematics Teacher* 100 (November 2006): 248–53.

3

Mathematics Instruction and Academic English: Adapting Problems for Varying English Proficiencies

Kerry Anne Enright

IN RECENT years, changes in mathematics standards and curricula increasingly emphasize attention to the *language* of mathematics learning and problem solving. Among the Process Standards in the 2000 NCTM mathematics standards is an emphasis on communication skills so that students can, among other things, "communicate their mathematical thinking coherently and clearly to peers, teachers, and others" and "use the language of mathematics to express mathematical ideas precisely" (NCTM 2000, p. 402). However, for many students, particularly students who speak languages other than English at home, the learning of mathematics is complicated by the language and literacy skills required to engage fully in classroom instruction and learning. This article presents guidelines for making the language of mathematics more accessible to *all* students, including students who are still learning English, with special attention to the language used when giving instructions and designing word problems.

Mathematics Instruction of English Language Learners

Content instruction that is adapted to be comprehensible to English language learners, or students for whom English is a second language, is known as Specially Designed Academic Instruction in English or sheltered instruction (Echevarria, Vogt, and Short 2000; Guarino et al. 2001). Handbooks, chapters, and other guides that offer sheltered strategies specifically for mathematics teachers include those by Anstrom (1999), Chamot and O'Malley (1994), Mather and Chiodo (1994), Buchanan and Helman (1993), and Wrigley (2001). Sheltered mathematics strategies focus on such aspects as a slower rate of speech, the use of visuals and manipulatives to support speech, delaying the use of certain kinds of abstract vocabulary, and presenting mathematics vocabulary in particular ways. Strategy-based resources from mathematics education experts examine the influences of culture and language on mathematics learning (Bresser 2003; Khisty 2002), and research-based articles recommend particular curricula or approaches to mathematics instruction for teachers of English language learners (Dalton and Sison 1995; Henderson and Landesman 1992; Khisty

Even as educators attempt to implement these myriad strategies to make their instruction more accessible to bilingual students, they sometimes do so with texts and materials that are still linguistically dense and difficult for many students to understand.

2002; Secada and Carey 1989). Even as educators attempt to implement these myriad strategies to make their instruction more accessible to bilingual students, they sometimes do so with texts and materials that are still linguistically dense and difficult for many students to understand. Often, the very language of instructions and mathematical problems is unnecessarily complex, preventing many students—not only English language learners—from understanding the task at hand. For example, nuances in forms of English, such as word choice and syntax, can complicate the meaning of a mathematical phrase or problem. Dale and Cuevas (1992) cite the vocabulary and language patterns in table 3.1 as potentially confusing examples of language that are typical in mathematics classrooms.

Table 3.1
Complicated Forms of Language in Mathematics

Vocabulary	**Syntax**
addition: *plus, combine, and, sum, increased by*	prepositions: eight *divided by* four and eight *into* four
subtraction: *subtract from, decreased by, less, minus, differ, less than, take away*	*greater than/less than*

The following guidelines will (1) help teachers identify the *language demands* of their instructions and word problems and (2) reduce those language demands so that the curriculum is more accessible to bilingual students, learners with reading difficulties, and young people with a variety of learning styles and mathematics abilities. Reducing the language demands of instructions and problems helps *all* students engage more immediately with the actual mathematical concepts rather than puzzle through complex language before engaging in the mathematics itself.

Reducing the Language Demands of Mathematics Problems: Guidelines

Teachers should also consider how to teach many of these demanding aspects of language to their students explicitly over time, so that, over the course of the year, materials need not be adapted to the same degree or in the same way.

These guidelines were developed to help teachers simplify the language of mathematics problems, or reduce their linguistic complexity. They are one set of tools that teachers can use to make their content more accessible to a broader range of students. A danger is present in using these guidelines without careful thought, however. Teachers who become adept at reducing the linguistic complexity of their instruction run the risk of leaving students ill-prepared to master the academic language of the discipline of mathematics. In other words, these guidelines provide greater *access* to the mathematical content and activities. Teachers should also consider how to teach many of these demanding aspects of language to their students explicitly over time, so that, over the course of the year, materials need not be adapted to the same degree or in the same way.

1. Use Active Voice at First

Often, academic texts use the passive voice to set up a problem or explain a process. The passive voice is used in the statement "The solution can be found by adding x and y." The same statement can be phrased in the active voice in several ways:

Find the solution by adding x and y.

Solve by adding x and y.

Add x and y to solve.

$x + y =$ _____.

Note the passive voice in the following statement: "Jon was given 6 apples. Sara was given 3." In the active voice, this statement can be rewritten as—

Jon had 6 apples. Sara had 3.

or

Jon received 6 apples. Sara received 3.

One exception to the "active voice" guideline involves the use of the phrase "is called," which is a very typical construction in academic English and is often unavoidable.

2. Use Simple Verb Tenses and Constructions

In mathematics problems and their instructions, use verbs in ways that make their meaning, and the students' task, as obvious as possible. Avoid complex verb tenses, such as "have had" or "were given," and avoid unnecessary modifiers in the instructions. See table 3.2 for a few examples of simplifying the use of verbs.

Table 3.2
Simplifying Verb Tense and Construction

Instead of ...	Try ...
Try to select ...	Select ...
Carefully explain ...	Explain ...
Give a detailed description ...	Describe ...

The following word problem has verb tenses that can be simplified:

Samuel was decorating the signs for the school car wash with 2 gallons of green paint. He also purchased 1/2 gallon of orange paint and 3 1/2 gallons of yellow paint. If each sign would require 1/4 gallon of paint, how many total signs could Samuel decorate?

Rewriting the problem with the following more simplified verb tenses makes it more comprehensible to a broader range of students:

> Samuel *has* 2 gallons of green paint to decorate signs for the school car wash. He also *has* 1/2 gallon of orange paint and 3 1/2 gallons of yellow paint. If each sign *requires* 1/4 gallon of paint, how many total signs *can* Samuel decorate?

3. Use Flow Charts and Graphic Organizers

Visual organizers and flow charts can help students follow a process or identify individual steps in a sequence to solve a problem, and they should be used with problems that have more than one approach, multiple steps, or embedded choices. Curricula that emphasize inquiry-based approaches to learning often prefer that students create such organizers on their own as part of their learning process. For students who are still learning English, as well as other students who are struggling readers, an exclusive emphasis on English text to engage with or understand a problem can prevent them from engaging with the problem at all. Under such circumstances, teachers can provide several types of organizers and ask students to select the correct one for the problem. For students who are very limited in their English, the teacher can point out the correct organizer to help the students get started.

The flow chart in figure 3.1 helps students solve quadratic equations. In many classes, students would benefit from having this flow chart extended even further to demonstrate how to solve by square roots, by factoring, and by using the quadratic formula. The flow chart could be posted on a wall with different sections printed on different colored paper for easy reference and "chunking" of the processes and steps involved in solving.

Even simple operations can appear complex to students with language and literacy problems if they are unfamiliar with the operation or lack the language abilities to follow multiple steps in a process. Flow charts and similar graphic organizers give them more immediate access to the operations being taught, without the need to interpret long chunks of language at the same time.

4. Incorporate Cognates

Many academic words in English are *cognates*, or words that look or sound similar across languages—especially words that share Latin roots with words in the Romance languages (Spanish, French, Italian, Portuguese). Students from Romance language backgrounds will have greater access to the language of mathematics problems if cognates are used in the text or materials. A list of some English-to-Spanish cognates is included in table 3.3. An important caveat to remember, however, is that Spanish-speaking students may understand the everyday meaning of a word in Spanish without fully understanding the academic meaning or expectations associated with the word.

Many academic words in English are *cognates*, or words that look or sound similar across languages—especially words that share Latin roots with words in the Romance languages (Spanish, French, Italian, Portuguese). Students from Romance language backgrounds will have greater access to the language of mathematics problems if cognates are used in the text or materials.

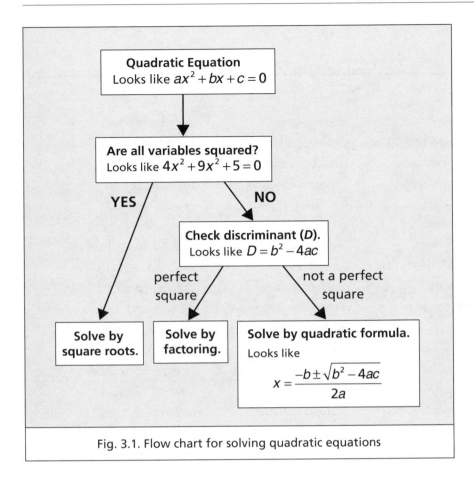

Fig. 3.1. Flow chart for solving quadratic equations

5. Avoid Introducing New Concepts or Processes and New Vocabulary Together

Students, especially bilingual students, have a great deal of difficulty grasping a concept they do not understand when it is explained only in language that they do not understand. Teachers can help students engage with new concepts more fruitfully by using as much familiar vocabulary as possible. Likewise, when new vocabulary is taught, a helpful tactic is to rely on familiar concepts and schemata when explaining the new vocabulary. Explaining new vocabulary by describing its meaning in several contexts (e.g., on a race track, at a carnival, at the supermarket) can be a useful teaching tool for native speakers of English. However, multiple scenarios can confuse English language learners even more if they do not have command of the vocabulary of those contexts. In such instances, the teacher should rely on scenarios and contexts that have been addressed in prior classes and units to ensure that *all* students have access to the new material being taught. Whenever possible, introduce new concepts with familiar vocabulary and cognates, and introduce new vocabulary with familiar concepts.

For example, consider a teacher who chooses to introduce concepts of probability in the classroom with a deck of cards. Even if bilingual students are very familiar with playing cards, they may be completely unaware of the everyday English vocabulary used in card playing. Consequently, they will have to learn two kinds of vocabulary simultaneously. That is, they will need

Whenever possible, introduce new concepts with familiar vocabulary and cognates, and introduce new vocabulary with familiar concepts.

33

Table 3.3
English-to-Spanish Cognates

Verbs	Nouns	Other
apply: aplicar	angle: ángulo	absolute: absoluto
approximate: aproximar	circle: círculo	certain: cierto
calculate: calcular	constant: constante	false: falso
compare: comparar	distance: distancia	finite: finito
cube: cubicar	fraction: fracción	general: general
define: definir	graph: gráfica	impossible: imposible
derive: derivar	inverse: inverso	improbable: improbable
determine: determinar	line: línea	minimal: mínimo
divide: dividir	number: número	parallel: paralelo
estimate: estimar	rectangle: rectángulo	plane: plano
explain: explicar	solution: solución	possible: posible
illustrate: ilustrar	sum: suma	prime: primo
include: incluir	symmetry: simetría	probable: probable
justify: justificar	table: tabla	rational: racional
predict: predecir	triangle: triángulo	real: real
represent: representar	vocabulary: vocabulario	simple: simple (sencillo)
select: seleccionar	volume: volumen	vertical: vertical

to know the vocabulary of playing cards, such as the names of the different suits (*hearts, spades, diamonds, clubs*); any verbs that might appear in an example or scenario, such as *shuffle, cut, deal;* and the names for the queen, king, jack, and ace. At the same time, the students must learn the content vocabulary related to probability, such as *likely, probable, conditional, complementary, permutation,* and *outcome.* To increase the likelihood that bilingual students have access to the *content vocabulary,* the teacher is wise to introduce the concepts in a scenario for which *all* students have already demonstrated a shared understanding of the language. For example, instead of starting with playing cards or games of chance, the teacher can introduce the concepts by talking about the probability of guessing the correct answer on a multiple-choice test question. Once all students understand both the *concepts* and the *vocabulary* of the new topic, the teacher can introduce new scenarios and their related vocabulary as interesting contexts for practice and further exploration of the basic concepts.

6. Simplify Sentence Structure

In some instances, fairly complex sentences cannot be avoided. In those instances, if possible, borrow language from past sections of text on the same page and teach students to refer to a part of the text (in the book or in an example on the board) in which that same phrase was used in a simpler context. Occasionally, simplifying sentence structure and avoiding too many new terms results in more language and longer text. Two simple sentences might be longer than one complex one—and that is acceptable! If complex constructions are necessary, the teacher should support their meaning with other visual and textual supports (e.g., images, tables, examples). An example of simplifying sentence structure can be seen in table 3.4.

Occasionally, simplifying sentence structure and avoiding too many new terms results in more language and longer text. Two simple sentences might be longer than one complex one—and that is acceptable!

Table 3.4
Simplifying Sentence Structure

Instead of ...	Try ...
Is the ratio of the area of a square to the area of the circle whose circumference is equal to the perimeter of the square always the same? Why or why not?	*Given:* The circumference of Circle "*C*" is equal to the perimeter of Square "*S*." Circumference of Circle "*C*" = *X*. Perimeter of Square "*S*" = *X*. ***True or False:*** The ratio of the area of Square "*S*" to the area of Circle "*C*" will ALWAYS be the same, for EVERY value of *X*. ***Why?***

7. Delay the Use of Pronouns

English language learners often have difficulty identifying the referent of pronouns in dense academic texts. In the beginning it is usually better to repeat the term rather than trust that students can find the referent on their own. For example, instead of writing or saying, "The perimeter of *ABCD* equals *that* of *ARST*," say, "The perimeter of *ABCD* equals *the perimeter* of *ARST*."

8. Repeat Patterns of Language, Then Paraphrase

In early instruction, when a pattern of language is introduced, try to repeat it so that students become familiar with the pattern. The next time this pattern of language appears, try to present a paraphrased version in close proximity. Repeat and paraphrase often so that students have many chances to master different ways of expressing the same idea or concept. See table 3.5 for an example.

9. Prioritize Vocabulary

Students who are still learning English are inundated with new vocabulary each day, from phrases about food in the cafeteria to discipline-specific terms in their content classrooms. Teachers can help English language learners by prioritizing high-frequency words and terms that are likely to appear in the future in class, on examinations, and in future courses. For obscure vocabulary that will not be used beyond the current unit of study,

Table 3.5
Repetition and Paraphrasing of Language Pattern

Instance of Use	*Example of Teacher Language*
First time	*The length of each side is an integer (not a fraction).*
Second time	*The length of each side is an integer (not a fraction).*
Third time	*The length of each side is an integer.*
Fourth time	*It has sides of integral length. (The length of each side is an integer).*
Fifth time	*It has sides of integral length.*
Sixth time	*… with sides of integral length (not a fraction).*

teachers can allow students access to a personal glossary or notebook. For example, if the teacher described in guideline 5 decides ultimately to focus his probability unit on games of chance, English language learners could be permitted during class work, homework, and tests to keep open an approved glossary of terms related to games of chance (with words like *spinner*, *die* or *dice*, and *shuffle*), even if the teacher wishes to exclude glossaries or study aids that include mathematical vocabulary related to probability.

10. Make the Language of Mathematics More Demanding over Time

By the end of the year, students should be exposed to language that is much closer to that of grade-level textbooks in your content area, and they should be prepared to understand it. This outcome will require spending extra time focusing explicitly on the language of mathematics and how it differs from language use in informal everyday settings. By methodically introducing students to the types of adaptations described above and modeling *how* the teacher has achieved that adaptation, he or she can prepare students to understand and adapt similar mathematical language more independently. As in developing mathematical understanding, however, linguistic understanding requires multiple opportunities for practice over time and depends on a foundation of prior skills. Mathematics teachers may find helpful a consultation with their school's English Language Development or English as a Second Language specialist to help determine the appropriate "language of mathematics" goals given the current English proficiencies of bilingual learners in their classrooms.

Summary

This article provides teachers with tools to make instructions and problems in mathematics classrooms accessible to a broader range of students by reducing their language demands. Ten guidelines address common sources of difficulty for English learners as they attempt to access written mathemati-

Teachers can help English language learners by prioritizing high-frequency words and terms that are likely to appear in the future in class, on examinations, and in future courses. For obscure vocabulary that will not be used beyond the current unit of study, teachers can allow students access to a personal glossary or notebook.

cal problems and their instructions, preparing teachers and researchers to adapt the language to make it more accessible to bilingual students. For more general instructional strategies to make mathematics instruction accessible to English learners, teachers should consult the referenced manuals and guidelines in this article's introduction that describe *sheltered* instructional techniques. The guidelines in this article are intended to support, supplement, or introduce teachers to sheltered instruction. They are not intended to replace a broader repertoire of teaching strategies for linguistically diverse students. However, these language guidelines will give the reader a deeper understanding of the linguistic demands of mathematics textbooks and materials and ways to reduce those linguistic demands as necessary.

REFERENCES

Anstrom, Kris. *Preparing Secondary Education Teachers to Work with English Language Learners: Mathematics.* Washington, D.C. National Clearinghouse for Bilingual Education, 1999.

Bresser, Rusty. "Helping English-Language Learners Develop Computational Fluency." *Teaching Children Mathematics* 9 (February 2003): 294–99.

Buchanan, Keith, and Mary Helman. *Reforming Mathematics Instruction for ESL Literacy Students.* Washington, D.C.: National Clearinghouse for Bilingual Education, 1993.

Chamot, Anna, and Michael O'Malley. *The CALLA Handbook: Implementing the Cognitive Academic Language Learning Approach.* Reading, Mass.: Addison-Wesley Publishing Co., 1994.

Dale, Theresa D., and Gilberto Cuevas. "Integrating Mathematics and Language Learning." In *The Multicultural Classroom: Readings for Content-Area Teachers*, edited by Patricia Richard-Amato and Marguerite Snow, pp. 330–48. White Plains, N.Y.: Longman, 1992.

Dalton, Stephanie, and June Sison. *Enacting Instructional Conversation with Spanish-Speaking Students in Middle School Mathematics.* Berkeley, Calif.: National Center for Research on Cultural Diversity and Second Language Learning, 1995.

Echevarria, Jana, Mary Ellen Vogt, and Deborah Short. *Making Content Comprehensible for English Language Learners: The SIOP Model.* Needham Heights, Mass.: Allyn & Bacon, 2000.

Guarino, Anthony J., Jana Echevarria, Deborah Short, J. E. Schick, S. Forbes, and Robert S. Rueda. "The Sheltered Instruction Observation Protocol." *Journal of Research in Education* 11, no. 1 (2001): 138–40.

Henderson, Ronald and Edward Landesman. *Mathematics and Middle School Students of Mexican Descent: The Effects of Thematically Integrated Instruction.* Reports Paper rr05. Berkeley, Calif.: Center for Research on Education, Diversity, and Excellence, 1992.

Khisty, Lena L. "Mathematics Learning and the Latino Student: Suggestions from Research for Classroom Practice." *Teaching Children Mathematics* 9 (September 2002): 32–35.

Mather, Jean R. C., and John J. Chiodo. "A Mathematical Problem: How Do We Teach Mathematics to LEP Elementary Students?" *Journal of Educational Issues of Language Minority Students* 13 (Spring 1994): 1–12.

National Council of Teachers of Mathematics (NCTM). *Principles and Standards for School Mathematics.* Reston, Va.: NCTM, 2000. standards.nctm.org/document/appendix/process.htm#bp3.

Secada, Walter G., and Deborah A. Carey. *Innovative Strategies for Teaching Mathematics to Limited English Proficient Students.* National Clearinghouse for Bilingual Education (NCBE) Program Information Guide Series, No. 10. Washington D.C.: NCBE, Summer, 1989.

Wrigley, Pamela. *The Help! Kit: A Resource Guide for Secondary Teachers of Migrant English Language Learners.* Oneonta, N.Y.: ESCORT (Eastern Stream Center on Resources and Training), 2001. www.escort.org/products/HSc1c12.pdf.

Help One, Help All

Julie Sliva Spitzer
Dorothy Y. White
Alfinio Flores

Now, more than ever before, mathematics teachers are asked to teach students more and better mathematics. When increased instructional demands are coupled with an increase in the diversity in our classrooms—including academic, cultural, linguistic, and socioeconomic diversity—teaching mathematics to all students is quite a challenge. Teachers may believe that they need to make an impossible number of accommodations and modifications to meet the individual needs of all their students. However, the task is less daunting when teachers implement strategies that are proved effective for students with a specific need and benefit other students as well. Teachers find that by helping one student understand mathematics through a particular approach, they also help all their students learn mathematics better. Teachers can employ simple strategies—using multiple representations, making connections, and promoting communication—to address the needs of specific students that will in turn serve all their students.

In this article we discuss the importance of creating a learning environment that fosters the development of every student's mathematical power. Next we present strategies that were initially designed to help one type of student (e.g., English language learners, special education students) but actually help all students learn mathematics. We close with a classroom example illustrating how the strategies can promote the mathematics learning of all students.

Create a Learning Environment to Foster Mathematical Development

The learning environment is the most important factor in fostering the mathematical development of all students. The environment communicates to students what "doing mathematics" means and what we value in the teaching-learning process. According to the National Council of Teachers of Mathematics (NCTM) (Martin 2007, pp. 39–40), "the teacher of mathematics should create a learning environment that provides—

- the time necessary to explore sound mathematics and deal with significant ideas and problems;
- a physical space and appropriate materials that facilitate students' learning of mathematics;

> **Teachers can employ simple strategies—using multiple representations, making connections, and promoting communication—to address the needs of specific students that will in turn serve all their students.**

39

- access and encouragement to use appropriate technology;

- a context that encourages the development of mathematical skill and proficiency;

- an atmosphere of respect and value for students' ideas and ways of thinking;

- an opportunity to work independently or collaboratively to make sense of mathematics;

- a climate for students to take intellectual risks in raising questions and formulating conjectures; and

- encouragement for [students] to display a sense of mathematical competence by validating and supporting ideas with a mathematical argument."

> **All students must have an opportunity to learn and develop a deep understanding of mathematics by participating in a supportive learning environment.**

All students must have an opportunity to learn and develop a deep understanding of mathematics by participating in a supportive learning environment. To achieve this goal, teachers must have knowledge of mathematics, knowledge of teaching strategies, and knowledge of their students.

In the following sections we address how teachers can create a supportive learning environment by getting to know their students, using multiple representations, making connections, and promoting active communication. Too often, students with special needs, English language learners, low-income, and minority students are not afforded an opportunity to engage in these types of environments. However, the strategies outlined in this article will not only make mathematics more accessible for more students but also provide an enriched experience for gifted and talented students, who are usually offered only the opportunity to learn the same content, just faster.

Get to Know Your Students on Many Levels

> **Often students whose backgrounds are different from their teachers' or peers' feel like strangers in school.**

Developing a positive relationship with your students begins with getting to know your students and the many facets of their lives. Often students whose backgrounds are different from their teachers' or peers' feel like strangers in school. The differences can be in terms of ethnic group, socioeconomic status, language, ability level, or life expectations. Teachers can help all students feel more like an integral part of school by becoming interested in them on many levels. Teachers can learn a great deal about their students by asking them what they like to do outside of school, their families, their celebrations, and their challenges.

Teachers can also talk to other people who can provide important insights about the student, such as parents and guardians, previous teachers, and in some cases, special education teachers, social workers, or English as a Second Language teachers. For example, a previous teacher may share the content the student mastered in a previous grade, how he or she preferred to learn mathematics, or how he or she worked with other students. However, teachers must determine whether the information matches what they notice as students engage in the mathematics classroom, to avoid any unintended misinformation about the student. By learning about students on many levels, teachers can include the students' backgrounds and interest in problems posed and establish better working relationships with students.

Use Multiple Representations

Using multiple representations involves presenting a concept in different ways to promote understanding among more students. For example, when teaching a new concept a teacher may use words, diagrams, concrete representations, graphs, equations, pictures, or symbolic representations. Most students need multiple ways of experiencing a concept to understand it fully. Some may prefer a verbal explanation; others may find that a visual representation helps them understand concepts better.

The concrete-representational-abstract (CRA) method is an instructional approach that research has found can facilitate the learning of students with learning disabilities (Harris, Miller, and Mercer 1995; Mercer and Miller 1992; Maccini and Gagnon 2000). This approach has three components: (1) concrete, in which the teacher models the concept in a concrete manner using manipulatives; (2) representational, in which the teacher transforms the concrete representation into a semiconcrete model, such as a drawing; and (3) abstract, in which the teacher models the previous representations in a symbolic manner using numbers and symbols. An example of this method is illustrated in the context of teaching the addition of fractions. The teacher may initially use pattern blocks to represent the concept concretely by combining blocks, then draw pictures of the pattern blocks to represent the addition in a semiconcrete manner, and finally move into solving a problem such as 1/2 + 1/6 abstractly. The CRA approach supports conceptual learning because it does not focus on the learning of "rules" and can benefit all types of learners.

Mathematical concepts are abstract, and using multiple representations can help students learn. Students should also be encouraged to represent their actions and thinking through multiple representations. The NCTM Representation Standard (NCTM 2000) suggests that students should increase the variety of their representations as they progress through school. More specifically, students in elementary school should represent objects they can see directly; in middle school students should represent objects they cannot see directly, such as rates or rational number; and finally in high school students should make representations of common mathematical structures (e.g., the sum of the first n odd natural numbers). By demonstrating concepts—especially new ones—concretely, pictorially, and symbolically *throughout* the grades, teachers can reach a variety of different learners and further their understanding. The most important point to remember however, is that students move through these different levels of representations at different paces.

Make Connections

Hiebert and Carpenter (1992) suggest that the number, accuracy, and strength of students' connections determine their degree of understanding. When

By demonstrating concepts—especially new ones—concretely, pictorially, and symbolically *throughout* the grades, teachers can reach a variety of different learners and further their understanding.

teaching students mathematics, connections need to be made among and within mathematics topics and with other subject areas (NCTM 2000). Students, especially those with learning difficulties, often have trouble making connections on their own and need support in making them (Bley and Thornton 1995; Clements 2000). Making connections explicit and helping students organize their knowledge of a mathematical topic are essential. One way these outcomes can be achieved is with concept maps (see figs. 4.1 and 4.2). Concept maps ask students to reflect on what they are learning and to make connections with new and existing knowledge. Encouraging students to engage in discussions about their maps and highlighting how different concepts, skills, and vocabulary are connected can strengthen the number of connections students can make.

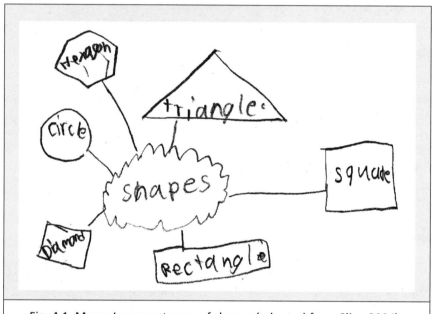

Fig. 4.1. Manny's concept map of shapes (adapted from Sliva 2004)

Teachers can also facilitate their students' mathematical connections by tying the content to their life experiences; the method for doing so may be different for each student. The different connections that students make will give their peers a rich network of examples of how mathematics can be relevant in different aspects of life. Students from groups that have not been served well by traditional approaches to mathematics may benefit from examples that make mathematics more relevant to their lives.

Students should also study how mathematics is used in the workplace. In a year-long project, algebra students were asked to find the mathematical concepts and processes they were studying in the workplace of community sponsors (Chazan and Bethel 1998). Students learned how quantities were measured or counted, what quantities were computed, how quantities were represented and related, and the type of comparisons used to compute quantities. Students were able to find places where the mathematics they were studying was used even in instances in which the spon-

The different connections that students make will give their peers a rich network of examples of how mathematics can be relevant in different aspects of life.

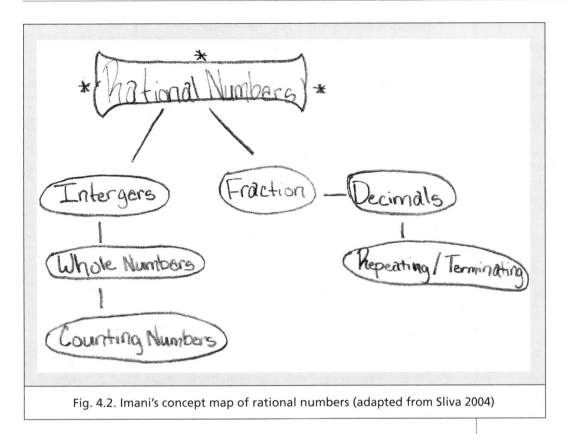

Fig. 4.2. Imani's concept map of rational numbers (adapted from Sliva 2004)

sors indicated that no mathematics was involved in their work. These students were able to see the relevance of algebraic concepts in very diverse workplaces.

Students tend to find mathematics more interesting and engaging if they perceive relevance to their lives. Helping students make connections, and having them come up with their own and then sharing with their peers, can help all students make more connections and derive more meaning from mathematical concepts.

Promote Active Communication

Establishing a classroom environment that invites all students to participate requires teachers to use various strategies that prompt students to understand and communicate their ideas. When teachers typically think of students who are challenged by communication, they think of students whose native language is not English. However, language barriers can also challenge special-education learners and students whose home language is not "academic English." These barriers may affect students' ability to receive knowledge or express their understandings. While students are explaining their thinking, they need to know that the use of their own words or modes of expression is acceptable. Sometimes these expressions will include the use of words in their native language or nonstandard English constructions. Students need to feel comfortable in sharing their ideas regardless of level of English proficiency or knowledge of academic terms.

Helping students make connections, and having them come up with their own and then sharing with their peers, can help all students make more connections and derive more meaning from mathematical concepts.

43

As students feel comfortable sharing their thoughts in their native language, teachers can begin to help them develop the academic English proficiency they will need to be successful throughout school.

As students feel comfortable sharing their thoughts in their native language, teachers can begin to help them develop the academic English proficiency they will need to be successful throughout school. These same skills are necessary to open many opportunities in life, and can be fostered by building on students' language rather than by repressing it. Students who are learning English as a second language are often able to communicate better in their first language, or by code switching, that is, by alternating between both languages in the same conversation. If teachers do not speak the language of the student, they can often obtain assistance from other students in the classroom who are bilingual. Students may also be allowed to use aids, such as manipulatives or drawings, to help them in communicating their understanding. In such an environment, other students, too, feel more freedom to express themselves mathematically using their own words.

Mathematical terms and concepts are not always easy to grasp. Teachers can support students by simplifying his or her own use of the language. Teachers can speak slowly, enunciate carefully, and write terms on the board or overhead projector in addition to speaking them. Rephrasing and emphasizing important mathematical ideas and concepts may benefit all students by focusing their attention on what they need to remember from the day's lesson. Spelling and pronunciation of technical terms in mathematics are also important to emphasize. Another strategy, word squares, has been used successfully by Winsor (2008) in working with his ELL students. In this strategy, students fold three-by-five-inch cards into four quadrants. In the respective quadrants, they write (1) the mathematical term in their own language, (2) the term in English, (3) the definition of the term in whichever language they understand, and (4) a representation of the concept. These strategies can benefit all students because they have a way to connect the new mathematical term with their current knowledge. By encouraging students to use the terms and important ideas as they share their ideas, teachers will ensure that all students have an opportunity to make connections and develop meaning and understanding of the mathematical terms being used.

Writing is another form of communication for students to share their ideas, reflect on their thoughts, and clarify their thinking. This strategy is particularly helpful for students who are not confident when speaking in front of others. Writing in the mathematics classroom can take the form of personal reflections or journaling. By providing this additional venue of communication to students who may not feel comfortable sharing verbally in the whole group, the teacher also benefits all students by giving them a tool to reflect and clarify their thoughts.

Students can also write using their peers as an audience. On such occasions, the teacher may make writing a public process. This writing will help students organize ideas so that they can be shared. The class can then discuss examples of students' writing. By trying to make sense of what others have written, readers will also develop a deeper understanding of the ideas being discussed.

Students may also need to communicate through gestures, body language, concrete materials, or drawings, especially when they want to convey meaning. The use of manipulative materials provides a concrete representation of the concept being taught and thus can support learners who have difficulties either processing the information as it comes in or those who are second-language learners and may have difficulties understanding the language.

We next present a classroom example that uses the strategies discussed in this article.

A Classroom Example: The Ice-Cream Survey

In the following scenario we offer a snapshot of a classroom focusing on a data-analysis project. After the short description, we address how each of the strategies we have previously discussed was used in this classroom.

The Problem

Mr. Reilly wanted to involve his fifth-grade students in selecting the ice-cream flavors for the annual end-of-year school picnic. He knew that his students loved ice cream and wanted to use this opportunity to assess their knowledge of collecting, analyzing, and representing data. The class was familiar with creating bar graphs and line plots from data presented in their textbooks. Mr. Reilly wanted to determine whether and how his students would apply these experiences in a real school example. He told the class that they needed to develop a plan for selecting the five flavors, and present their findings in multiple ways to convince him of the types and amounts of ice cream he needed to buy and why.

Brainstorming the Process

Mr. Reilly asked the class how they should go about solving the problem. At first students thought it was best to ask their friends and siblings what types of ice cream they liked, and then buy those types of ice cream. However, one student thought that a better approach would be to ask the students in each homeroom and to write down the types of ice cream they liked. Mr. Reilly restated the plan by saying, "So it sounds like you want to conduct a survey of the different homerooms." The class agreed. Mr. Reilly wrote the word *survey* on the board for the class to see.

As students thought about the survey, they cut slips of paper and wrote the question "What is your favorite ice cream?" Mr. Reilly realized that the class needed some guidance for creating the survey because the nature of their question would yield too many answers. So he suggested that the class conduct a survey in the room to test it out. Students selected all kinds of flavors and quickly realized that they needed a way to narrow down the choices. They decided on the top five flavors and modified their survey papers to read, "What is your favorite ice cream? Pick one: vanilla, chocolate, strawberry, rocky road, or mint chocolate chip." The class was then split into four groups to work on various aspects of the project. Mr. Reilly wanted to make sure that all students participated, so he added a role and responsibilities for each group. The groups, along with the roles, are delineated in the following list:

1. Create a survey for each homeroom to fill out that states the number of students who like the type of ice cream. (Each student votes once.) Role and responsibilities of the students: Survey Maker

2. Count the responses from each homeroom. Role and responsibilities of the students: Data Collector

3. Analyze the data to determine how much of each type of ice cream should be bought. Role and responsibilities of the students: Data Cruncher

4. Decide how much of each kind of ice cream they would like to order. Role and responsibilities of the students: Final Data Reporter

Mr. Reilly guided the classes' explorations through his questioning. At each point in the lesson, he prompted students to come up with a plan to determine how much of what type of ice cream should be bought. He reminded them that they needed to record their results in multiple ways and to determine how much they would need to buy and why. Mr. Reilly carefully monitored the process and provided feedback to the students as they worked to achieve their goal.

The final product required that the students take turns "reporting out" to the teacher and the entire class, both verbally and in writing, about how and why their group made their decisions. For example, the group who had task 1 described how they created the survey so that each homeroom got only one sheet. They defended their choice using numbers (e.g., number of sheets for each class versus number of sheets for each student) and diagrams (e.g., copies of survey sheets). A written description of each of their components was included in the final report to the teacher. Each student was responsible for his or her part as well as understanding the entire project. This requirement was evidenced in a verbal question-and-answer session in which the teacher asked students about aspects of the project for which they were not directly responsible. The students were also required to respond in their journals to specific questions about the experience. These questions were different for each student, but the students did not know about the variation.

Discussion

In this example, Mr. Reilly was focusing on a variety of different aspects of teaching. First, he was interested in involving *all* his students in learning mathematics by tying the experience to something they were all interested in—ice cream. He did so as a means of creating a learning environment that was engaging for all. In this process his students worked collaboratively and selected tasks that they felt comfortable participating in, although ultimately they were responsible for understanding each piece of the project and the final conclusion.

Students were required to use multiple representations of data to convince Mr. Reilly of how much ice cream to buy and why. Some used diagrams, drew pictures, or completed bar and circle graphs. Others crunched numbers, such as mean, median, and mode, or used proportional thinking to explain their answers. All students had to think of different ways to explain their answers. Note that the students used only representation and abstract means to share their ideas. None of them used concrete models because they had developed conceptual understanding and thus had moved to more sophisticated ways of representation.

In addition to connections made with their lives, connections were made among and between other concepts, skills, and areas of mathematics and other subject areas. The students used counting, comparing, analyzing, reasoning, problem solving, and data analysis in this project. These connections allowed Mr. Reilly to note the strength and accuracy of students' mathematical understanding.

Throughout this lesson the students were consistently engaged in the project and communicating their ideas. First, they had to work together as a class to determine a process by which they were going to solve the ice-cream issue. Next they worked in smaller groups to complete their tasks. Ultimately they went back to working with the entire group to complete the final question-and-answer and write-up. As stated previously, students were permitted to choose their groups, so they could join others they felt most comfortable with or perhaps could work with a student who complemented their best efforts. When they presented their part, they were allowed to do so with their group so that no one individual was singled out. Students were encouraged to use multiple ways to demonstrate their findings so that use of the written language was not the sole avenue to demonstrate what they understood.

Mr. Reilly designed this entire project to help all his students learn mathematics. In designing an activity that would engage all his learners, he promoted a positive learning environment, the use of multiple representations, connections with other areas inside and outside mathematics, and communication among his students.

Summary

The strategies presented in this article are grounded in the NCTM Process Standards (NCTM 1991, 2000) of Representation, Connections, and Communication. We chose these standards to emphasize the importance of using a variety of teaching strategies to teach mathematics to *all* students. Such strategies as learning about your students, fostering a positive learning environment, using multiple representations, and making connections underscore the belief that all students can learn. If a teacher believes that all his or her students can learn, then determining how students learn best and using alternative instructional approaches that capitalize on how students learn best is a must. Our hope is that you, too, believe, that all your students can and will learn mathematics, just in different ways and at different times.

REFERENCES

Bley, Nancy S., and Carol A. Thornton. *Teaching Mathematics to Students with Learning Disabilities.* 4th ed. Austin, Tex.: Pro-Ed, 2001.

If a teacher believes that all his or her students can learn, then determining how students learn best and using alternative instructional approaches that capitalize on how students learn best is a must.

Chazan, Daniel, and Sandra C. Bethell. "Working with Algebra." In *High School Mathematics at Work*, edited by Mathematical Sciences Education Board, pp. 35–41. Washington D.C.: National Academies Press, 1998.

Clements, Douglas H. "Translating Lessons from Research into Mathematics Classrooms: Mathematics and Special Needs Students." *Perspectives* 26, no. 3 (2000): 31–33.

Harris, Carolyn A., Susan P. Miller, and Cecil D. Mercer. "Teaching Initial Multiplication Skills to Students with Disabilities in General Education Classrooms." *Learning Disabilities Research and Practice* 10, no. 3 (Summer 1995): 180–95.

Hiebert, James, and Thomas P. Carpenter. "Learning and Teaching with Understanding." In *Handbook of Research on Mathematics Teaching and Learning*, edited by Douglas A. Grouws, pp. 65–97. New York: Macmillan, 1992.

Maccini, Paula, and Joseph Calvin Gagnon. "Best Practices for Teaching Mathematics to Secondary Students with Special Needs." *Focus on Exceptional Children* 32, no. 5 (2000): 1–22.

Martin, Tami S., ed. *Mathematics Teaching Today: Improving Practice, Improving Student Learning*. 2nd ed. Reston, Va.: National Council of Teachers of Mathematics, 2007.

Mercer, Cecil D., and Susan P. Miller. "Teaching Students with Learning Problems in Math to Acquire, Understand, and Apply Basic Math Facts." *Remedial and Special Education* 13, no. 3 (May-June 1992): 19–35, 61.

National Council of Teachers of Mathematics (NCTM). *Professional Standards for Teaching Mathematics*. Reston, Va.: NCTM, 1991.

———. *Principles and Standards for School Mathematics*. Reston, Va.: NCTM, 2000.

Sliva, Julie A. *Teaching Inclusive Mathematics to Special Learners, K–6*. Thousand Oaks, Calif.: Corwin Press, 2004.

Winsor, Matthew S. "Bridging the Language Barrier in Mathematics." *Mathematics Teacher* 101, no. 5 (December 2007): 372–78.

Yes, You Can:
Teaming to Support Lower-Attaining Students in Accessing Algebra

Sandie Gilliam
Megan E. Staples
Jennifer Roberts Lahey

IN 1975, I, Sandie Gilliam, began teaching and, like many new mathematics teachers, was given a schedule of teaching the lowest-ability students in the high school even though I was the only teacher of ten in the mathematics department with a mathematics degree. The students in these classes had been unsuccessful in mathematics for years and had a weak foundation to support learning. Consequently these students disliked mathematics and therefore sometimes presented discipline problems in the classroom.

That first year I began to hypothesize about the teaching and learning of underachievers. Many teachers do not want to teach "those students." Often such students, because they have not yet mastered basic skills, are given the same content with the same teaching and learning techniques over and over again. With many high schools having a two-year mathematics requirement, most of these students would not choose the opportunity to learn the wonderful breadth and beauty of mathematics that exist beyond a fundamental course in algebra. I believed that things needed to be different.

Over the years, I continued to work with a variety of ability levels, and yet I maintained a passion for working with underachievers. One of my principals described me as a scientist, always experimenting. I tried new curricula or wrote my own; explored different classroom pedagogy and techniques; and collaborated with colleagues and researchers, discussing and studying teaching and learning. Thirty-one years later, I have just finished another year, teaching the three lowest ninth-grade mathematics classes at my school. One class in particular became the "experimental" class of this year. This class, which is the focus of this article, resulted from combining two mathematics classes—a low-level Math A, precollege-preparatory mathematics class and a special education mathematics class—in an effort to provide this group of students with the best instruction we could to support their growth and their development of number sense and algebraic reasoning.

A Collaborative Endeavor

The remainder of this article is the product of collaboration among the three authors as we brought our various perspectives and expertise to the analysis of teaching and learning that happened in this "experimental" class. Jennifer Lahey cotaught with Sandie. Jennifer is a credentialed special education teacher with a limited mathematics background. She is expected to be knowledgeable in many disciplines, including mathematics, science, English, social studies, and health, so that she can assist special education students in understanding course material. Megan Staples is a mathematics education researcher who has worked closely with Sandie on several projects, including analyzing videotapes of Sandie's lessons with several Math A classes over the years.

> **By examining this particular case—a combined low-level and special education class—and the instructional approach we found effective with this group, we offer some productive suggestions and a vision of working with low-attaining students that supports the development of their algebraic reasoning and conceptual understanding of mathematics.**

By examining this particular case—a combined low-level and special education class—and the instructional approach we found effective with this group, we offer some productive suggestions and a vision of working with low-attaining students that supports the development of their algebraic reasoning and conceptual understanding of mathematics. The challenges of course were many—the students demonstrated weak arithmetic skills and number sense; underdeveloped student skills and study habits; a wide range of learning styles and special needs; and, at least initially, negative attitudes toward mathematics and their own mathematical abilities. Through teaming, using tried-and-true methods, and experimenting, we were able to engage students in algebraic reasoning, sense making, and conceptual mathematics.

The Experimental Class

The experimental class started as two mathematics classes. Sandie's Math A class had twenty-one students who were both regular education and special education students. Their learning issues consisted of attention deficit with hyperactivity disorder, a variety of mild learning disabilities, speech and language impairments, hearing and visual impairments, emotional disturbances, and autism. Jennifer's Math 9–12 class comprised ten special education students with more significant needs who would take Math A the following year. Her students' learning difficulties included the above as well as moderate to severe learning disabilities, traumatic brain injury, and other health impairments.

Before school started, Sandie asked Jennifer if she might like to combine the two classes. The advantages might be the following:

- The Math 9–12 students (all in special education) would be mainstreamed into the least restrictive environment.

- All students would learn new material, with a review of basic skills embedded as those skills pertained to the new concepts.

- All Math 9–12 students would be exposed to new mathematics concepts and would have another opportunity to learn them in more depth the next year. Math 9–12 students who mastered the material would receive Math A credit and move to the next level.

- Math A students with Individual Education Plans (IEPs), as well as students with weaker mathematical skills who were *not* specifically targeted for additional support, would benefit from the collaboration. (Many

students had IEPs and a history working with Jennifer on a range of issues, including reading, writing, and attention issues that affect performance in mathematics.)

- Students would have three adults to support them in the classroom (a mathematics teacher, a special education teacher, and a paraprofessional).

- Jennifer would learn more mathematics content and pedagogy from Sandie, and Sandie would learn more special education techniques and strategies from Jennifer.

The disadvantages might be the following:

- Math 9–12 students might "slow down" the class and limit the scope of what could be accomplished with the Math A students alone.

- Math 9–12 students might feel inferior to the others.

- A larger class size might bring increased challenges.

- Students might discount Jennifer as a mathematics teacher and think of her as an adult aide.

We believed that overall it looked like a win-win situation for everyone, but we agreed that if at any time either of us thought it was not working, we would go back to the original design of separate classes. As the idea took shape, Jennifer thought it was important to discuss the plan with her class and their parents. Their reactions varied, but ultimately all were supportive of, and enthusiastic toward, the change. Her students were initially apprehensive, but they responded positively to the fact that they would be in a "normal" mathematics class. In talking with parents, Jennifer explained the changes and emphasized that the parents would need to play an important role in the mathematical education of their children this year and thus that communication and support at home would be crucial.

The Class

In addition to the wide range of learning styles and learning differences, the students in this combined class had a broad range of mathematical foundations. At the beginning of the year, more than half the students could be seen using their fingers to do their basic skills, and some were quite fast at it! Most students had scored Far Below Basic on the California Math Standards test for eighth-grade general mathematics the previous year. A few students had taken prealgebra and received a mediocre grade, and their parents thought that their child should have a stronger foundation before taking Algebra 1.

Regarding exposure to various mathematical topics, some students had worked with the order of operations, integers, solving equations, and basic graphing ideas. All students had experienced a plethora of work with basic mathematics skills. None had worked with a graphing calculator or encountered topics with polynomials, including multiplying binomials, and years had passed since they had had experiences with patterns. This emphasis on basic skills and lack of variety in mathematical topics

One common belief is that students who have not yet mastered their basic skills cannot be successful with mathematics that demands higher levels of reasoning, such as generalizing, problem solving, and justification. Some teachers shy away from engaging students with these topics. We took a different approach with this group.

is not an atypical curricular diet afforded students who are identified as performing below grade level (Oakes 2005). One common belief is that students who have not yet mastered their basic skills cannot be successful with mathematics that demands higher levels of reasoning, such as generalizing, problem solving, and justification. Some teachers shy away from engaging students with these topics. We took a different approach with this group.

Another important characteristic of this group was that few students had experienced success with mathematics. They brought with them negative attitudes toward the subject and little confidence in their abilities. They were aware that they were assigned to one of the school's lowest-level classes, and thus the institution reinforced that, at least relative to their peers, they were not mathematically successful. This perception played out in resistant attitudes toward participation, negative comments directed at peers and themselves, and a "can't do" approach to mathematics.

The Approach: A Focus on Sense Making

With the wide range of our students' mathematical foundations, their mathematics phobia, and their lack of a can-do attitude toward mathematics, our pedagogy and teaching materials had to be new and different. Past experiences and research indicated that we needed to focus on sense making and extending students' reasoning. In an effort to make learning easier, many educators break down the mathematics—they offer students "rules of thumb" to guide the students' work, or they reduce mathematics to a finite set of options or steps. In our experience, exactly the opposite approach is beneficial! Particularly for students with learning disabilities related to memory, the requirement to memorize a slew of facts, rules, and procedures is most challenging and frustrating. We have found that understanding is the essential element. Students, regardless of their particular learning differences, can think. If they are presented material that makes sense to them, *they* can turn this sense making into formulas and procedures. Math has a logical structure and coherence, and it can make sense to all students if we give them the means and time to do this work.

Students, regardless of their particular learning differences, can think. If they are presented material that makes sense to them, they can turn this sense making into formulas and procedures. Math has a logical structure and coherence, and it can make sense to all students if we give them the means and time to do this work.

Effective instruction depended on being responsive to students' thinking. It required that we listen carefully to the students as they asked questions and explained their thinking. We needed to diagnose who knew what, how it had been presented previously, and what learning styles worked best for each student and the class as a whole. We needed to establish a classroom environment in which the exchange of ideas was valued; in which question-asking was encouraged, both among peers and of the teacher; and in which students felt free to come to the board to explain their answers to problems, even if they had partial or wrong answers. Without this environment, students' ideas and reasoning would remain hidden from us. Although important in teaching all students, this approach is perhaps even more crucial when working with students who have unanticipated gaps in their backgrounds and who may think in rather nonstandard ways.

The Curricular Materials

We used the *Interactive Mathematics Program Year 1* (IMP 1) textbook (Fendel et al. 1997) as the foundation of the course and supplemented it in response to what the students needed. Two features of this textbook made it particularly appropriate for the sense-making work we aimed to do. First, IMP presents mathematics in a context and in relation to a "big question" or chapter theme. Students are introduced to the context and theme at the beginning of a unit and continue to use this context to reason about the mathematics and reflect on what they have done to determine whether it makes sense. For example, when working on graphing in the Overland Trail unit, students use the context of a journey across the country to produce and analyze graphs. Students draw on the situation to help them think through relationships among different quantities, and they move back and forth between context and more formal mathematics (Schroeder and Lester 1989).

The use of context allowed us to introduce mathematics topics using a more concrete or hands-on approach. Many special education students are kinesthetic learners. Given manipulatives, they can think as they play around with the materials, and they develop approaches and procedures that make sense to them. Hands-on work started most new topics, followed by drawing, and then tying the concept to more traditional-looking mathematics. This "tying" was a process of building on students' thinking and helping them progressively mathematize their reasoning and develop the means to represent that reasoning using standard mathematical symbols and conventions (Gravemeijer and van Galen 2003).

Second, the IMP book differs from other textbooks in that it requires students to read lengthier passages about problem situations. Many teachers and parents think using such reading-intensive curricular materials is not advisable, particularly considering this population, many of whom had low reading abilities and were supported by a special reading class. We disagree strongly. "Reading in the content area" is a necessary skill for everyone to develop. Mathematics is not solely about numbers; it is about real-life situations in which one needs to use mathematics to solve a problem. Most of our students will find themselves in situations in which they need to access text-based information, perhaps reading job manuals for instructions or newspaper articles to learn about important voter issues.

Leveraging the "Teaming"

Successful teaming occurs when colleagues share the workload and responsibilities, each taking the lead in the strength she offers. Similar classroom norms and behavioral expectations are also crucial. Perhaps most important, communication is vital. We often communicated in the evening, to discuss students' issues or plan lessons, prepare assignments and assessments, and attend to special education issues as needed. Teaming allowed us to be more responsive to the students and gave us a broader range of instructional strategies to draw on, or create, to reach them.

Hands-on work started most new topics, followed by drawing, and then tying the concept to more traditional-looking mathematics. This "tying" was a process of building on students' thinking and helping them progressively mathematize their reasoning and develop the means to represent that reasoning using standard mathematical symbols and conventions (Gravemeijer and van Galen 2003).

Modifying Materials

We worked together on many items that we sent back and forth as e-mail attachments so each could edit or add to the material. In particular, Jennifer would scaffold the assignments in light of her students' issues, many times creating review materials and practice sheets so that the students could understand what was being asked of them. The Math A students benefited greatly from these modifications as well. Furthermore, as Jennifer created these materials, she deepened her own understanding of the mathematics concepts as she thought about how to modify the work appropriately.

Leading the Class

In the classroom, we both led discussions of previous material, but Sandie took the lead in introducing new mathematics concepts. In this approach, students saw both of us as teachers, but Jennifer had the opportunity to master the new concept with its matching pedagogy before she needed to take the lead. At times, we interrupted each other when we observed that students appeared perplexed or needed another way of looking at or working the problem, or observed that one student had an innovative way of doing the problem. Throughout the year *rotations* were set up in which both teachers and the aide would lead and reinforce various concepts with small groups in different locations of the classroom. This arrangement was another way to differentiate instruction as needed.

Discipline

Discipline was also shared. The teacher leading the lesson maintained the instructional focus while the other one took the lead in monitoring the classroom, handling the discipline, and checking to determine that all the students were on task. With proximity, eye contact, or gentle touches on the shoulders, the class knew that an adult was always around, so problematic situations were rare. The classroom environment needed to be conducive to learning, especially because of special education issues related to hearing loss, auditory and visual processing impairments, and emotional disturbances, as well as a multitude of other difficulties.

Making Sense of Algebra

In this section, we look at how three particular topics were approached during the year. We focus on the strategies we used to support this group of lower-attaining students in making sense of the concepts related to these foundational algebraic ideas.

Integers

Our approach to integers focused on sense making. Often students arrive at high school with many a rule turned around. "Two negatives make a positive" is one such rule. When asked to explain, most students do not understand that this "rule" is dependent on the operation being used. Students do not have a conceptual understanding of positive and negative

numbers. The IMP book uses the notion of "hot and cold cubes" being added into a pot. Although this analogy is helpful for many students, kinesthetic learners need to touch objects. We used red and blue chips, letting the red ones represent the negatives, or "in the red" budgeting ideas, and the blue represent the positives. Students learned that the combination of red and blue makes a "neutral," or is worth "nothing." Eventually, they transferred this kinesthetic work with the chips to drawing pictures of what they were doing. Over time, this growth resulted in each student's figuring out and making sense of the rules for integer operations. If students forgot a rule, they always had a way to recreate it or to solve the specific problem. They were permitted to ask for a bag of chips at any time, including in classroom testing situations.

On a related note, we have found that the use of *color* is a powerful tool in helping underachievers learn by helping them visually differentiate and focus on ideas that in symbolic form could appear as numbers and variables that all blend together. Sandie first hypothesized about this effect when looking for a particular mathematics resource on her shelf of hundreds of titles. She realized that she searched for books by visualizing their color and size. With those attributes in mind, she could locate a particular book in a matter of seconds. She wondered whether color (along with size) was an added "sense" for enabling students to engage with algebra topics, especially integers, polynomials, and solving equations. Indeed, that seemed to be true.

Solving Equations

Solving equations can also be approached in a natural, more kinesthetic way: the balance scale. We started this concept with Jennifer acting as the scale, blue and red multilink cubes representing the integers, and blue and red plastic cups representing x or $-x$. Throughout the year we kept up the blue-and-red idea, which then reinforced and reviewed the previous use. "Do unto one side what you do unto the other" was a frequent mantra from us, and then the students, in response to the balancing-equations idea, would come up to Jennifer's arms and add or subtract cubes and cups. In turn, Jennifer's arms would model what was happening to the balance scale. The students understood that the goal was to get the cup (blue x) by itself on one side of the scale so that one could see what the value of x was by looking at the other side.

Eventually the students drew pictures of what was happening, often using colored pencils, instead of relying on the cubes and cups. As time went on, we transitioned to making the problem look more algebraic in nature, having students use only integers and symbols and showing their work as they went along—more like what they would be asked to do in an Algebra 1 class. Again, students knew they could ask for chips and cups if they needed to redevelop the idea at any time.

The Concept of a Variable

For many students, underachievers in particular, working with variables in algebra is a source of difficulty. Typically, in the first weeks of a prealgebra course, students work with x by substituting numerical values into expressions (e.g., let $x = 2$; find $4x + 1$) or by solving simple equations (e.g., find x if $4x + 1 = 13$), often using a guess-and-check strategy. In this approach, x serves as a number to be found. This role of x in algebra is different from the role x has when it represents a variable, that is, when the values of x truly vary (Kieran 1989). This understanding is crucial to later uses of variable in graphing lines and polynomials and representing relationships among quantities, such as required in setting up word problems. Our approach was to develop the variable x conceptually by working with patterns *before* students focused on substitution and solving equations.

We began by having students look for patterns in a "guess my rule" approach, for example, by making a simple in-out chart like the one seen in figure 5.1. Students must determine what to do to the In value to get the Out value.

In	Out
2	3
10	11
51	52
5	
0	
	12

Fig. 5.1. An example of an in-out chart

As a first step, a student volunteer was called on to fill in one of the empty cells, which then gave other students more clues. After filling in the table, students express the rule in words using the terms "In" and "Out." For this example, students might state, "take the 'In' number and add 1, and you get the 'Out' number." Students must have the freedom to use their own words, and the teacher should write the words exactly as the student has expressed them. The goal is to create a bridge from students' current understanding to more formalized mathematics, which happens when they have the opportunity to work from their current understanding.

A prerequisite to representing a pattern is seeing a pattern. Although patterns are part of the elementary school experience, this class had difficulty identifying patterns and generating other numbers in the pattern. The students found the process of looking for possibilities and then seeing when to eliminate an idea quite challenging. Perhaps equally important, they had not expected to have to do so. They thought the answer would readily appear, without their having to contemplate various patterns. In class, we called this process "troubleshooting." We likened it to the situation of an electronics repairperson who has to troubleshoot ideas until an appliance works. The appliance cannot talk and tell him what to do. He has to try a few ideas out and eliminate those that do not work. This analogy seemed to help the students understand the nature of the process of looking for a pattern and to gain confidence in tackling the problems.

Students must have the freedom to use their own words, and the teacher should write the words exactly as the student has expressed them. The goal is to create a bridge from students' current understanding to more formalized mathematics, which happens when they have the opportunity to work from their current understanding.

After many "guess my rules" (for which only positive integers occur in the table), we transitioned to having students shorten their verbal descriptions of the rule. Using the example above, a student might state, "In plus one equals Out." For students having a hard time moving to this step, we accepted the longer sentence version and then asked another student in class to shorten the sentence. The final transition occurred when the students replaced the In/Out values with x or y in the table and the words *In plus one equals Out* with the symbols $x + 1 = y$.

For each transition, the new step was written directly below the previous so that all students could see the important words and different components being preserved, modified, condensed, or dropped. Scaffolding these transitions is about helping students make sense of algebra and its notation by using number sense to see and represent patterns, then formulating these generalizations symbolically.

Later on in the course, after working with negative numbers, we go back to "guess my rule" using positive and negative values for x and y. Revisiting "guess my rule" refreshes and reinforces what they learned earlier and gives the students time to work first on seeing patterns and writing equations, without the extra encumbrance of negative numbers. We also explore how, for example, $2x - 1 = y$ is the same as $2x + (-1) = y$, as different students come up with these two seemingly different rules. An understanding of this equivalence seems to occur more naturally with this approach than when students are taught to rely on the rule "change the 'subtract 1' to 'add -1.'" Again, for these students, understanding, not memorizing rules, is the goal.

Reflections on the Experimental Class

The year seemed to be a success. Mathematically, we were able to engage students in many core algebraic topics in meaningful ways and support them in attaining a solid foundation. Some of the topics we addressed, in addition to those mentioned above, were the order of operations; simplifying expressions; writing an equation given the rate of change and the starting amount; using a graphing calculator to enter data or tables and graphing that information to predict other outcomes; and, given a situation in words, mathematically and logically solve the problem.

The students seemed to thrive as well. Several of Jennifer's students turned out to be leaders in the class. Of the ten who were enrolled, five were potential candidates for successfully completing the class and continuing on to Math B. Ultimately, three achieved this goal. The remainder would repeat the class the following year.

In their end-of-year portfolios, students commented on their experiences. Here are quotes from one student, taken as they were written.

> Algebra is sort of everything wrapped into one. The entire math that we learned in the past is added into algebra with some exponents and PEMDAS. Algebra has helped me into balancing things out. It is different because it is more complicated and has more rules to it then [sic] the more basic math

Mathematically, we were able to engage students in many core algebraic topics in meaningful ways and support them in attaining a solid foundation.

that I had learned. It teaches us logic and reasoning. It is used in common solving but the process is important because you learn problem solving and reasoning.

I think algebra is a lot easier this year then [sic] it was last year. It was easier because I had someone to teach me several ways and go over it with me. I hardly every had to go to my parents for help. (AP)

For Sandie and Jennifer, team-teaching the class was also a valuable growth experience. They learned from each other. Sandie, trained as a mathematics teacher, learned from Jennifer about different learning disabilities, how students learn to compensate for them, and what teachers still need to do to support—not enable—the students as they tackle more difficult material. Jennifer, trained as a special education teacher, benefited from Sandie's immense mathematics background and knowledge and her sensitivity to the fact that Jennifer would be teaching some material in the class for the first time. Jennifer also valued the inquiry-based questioning and unit progressions that involved so many "ah-ha" moments for the students. "They have left me with a lifetime of strategies that have made me a better teacher."

The challenges of offering lower-attaining students authentic access to algebraic thinking and mathematics are many. Bringing multiple lenses to the classroom and teaching in a way that is responsive to students' ideas and needs can open up new paths to success.

REFERENCES

Fendel, Dan, and Diane Resek, with Lynne Alper and Sherry Fraser. *Interactive Mathematics Program Year 1: Integrated High School Mathematics*. Berkeley, Calif.: Key Curriculum Press, 1997.

Gravemeijer, Keono, and Frans van Galen. "Facts and Algorithms as Products of Students' Own Mathematical Activity." In *A Research Companion to* Principles and Standards for School Mathematics, edited by Jeremy Kilpatrick, W. Gary Martin, and Deborah Schifter, pp. 114–22. Reston, Va.: National Council of Teachers of Mathematics, 2003.

Kieran, Carolyn. "The Early Learning of Algebra: A Structural Perspective." In *Research Issues in the Learning and Teaching of Algebra*, edited by Sigrid Wagner and Carolyn Kieran, pp. 33–56. Reston, Va.: National Council of Teachers of Mathematics, 1989.

Oakes, Jeannie. *Keeping Track: How Schools Structure Inequality*. 2nd ed. New Haven, Conn.: Yale University Press, 2005.

Schroeder, Thomas L., and Frank K. Lester Jr. "Developing Understanding in Mathematics via Problem Solving." In *New Directions for Elementary School Mathematics*, 1989 Yearbook of the National Council of Teachers of Mathematics (NCTM), edited by Paul R. Trafton and Albert P. Shulte, pp. 31–42. Reston, Va.: NCTM, 1989.

Using a "New Synthesis of Reading in Mathematics" to Encourage Disadvantaged High School Students to Act Like a Community of Mathematicians

Janet St. Clair
Jamye Witherspoon Carter
Sibyl Yvette St. Clair

THE increasingly diverse classroom has encouraged educators to reflect more deeply on ways to develop interesting lessons that have the potential to promote rich mathematical classroom communication, conceptual understanding, connections among the different fields of mathematics, connections between mathematics and other disciplines, and an awareness of the human side of mathematics and its growth and change over time. Raffaella Borasi's and Marjorie Siegel's "new synthesis of reading in mathematics" (Siegel, Borasi, and Smith 1989; Siegel and Borasi 1992; Borasi and Siegel 2000) has great potential to accomplish these ideas in *any* classroom. Reading is particularly suitable for diverse classrooms for several reasons. For example, it is cost-effective and can expose students to a wide range of mathematics-related ideas that are interesting, experientially real to them, or "tap into" their world.

Borasi (a mathematics educator) and Siegel (a reading educator) combine a variety of mathematics texts (e.g., the standard school textbook; essays and articles about the history, philosophy, and applications of mathematics; novels or stories about mathematics; newspaper articles; student-authored works) with reading strategies guided by Rosenblatt's (1938, 1978) transactional reading strategy. Under the transactional view of reading, the reader's prior experiences, experiences while reading (e.g., thoughts or feelings, questions raised), and the context in which the text is read play a part in the reader's interpretation of the text. The reader actually negotiates the author's intended message with his or her interpretation of the text. Reading is viewed as an exciting "exploration" in which meanings vary across readers and within readers (Borasi et al. 1998).

Three reading strategies that Borasi and Siegel have employed include *say something, cloning an author,* and *sketch-to-sketch.* The "say something" strategy involves reading a text in pairs and stopping at points determined by the readers (e.g., at the end of a sentence, at the end of a paragraph) to engage in such activities as asking questions, explaining, predicting what will happen next, relating to a previous experience, and making connections with other texts and contexts (Harste, Pierce, and

Reading is particularly suitable for diverse classrooms for several reasons.

Reading is viewed as an exciting "exploration" in which meanings vary across readers and within readers (Borasi et al. 1998).

Cairney 1985, cited in Borasi and Siegel 1990). This strategy helps students feel a sense of ownership of the text as they monitor their own reading and reflect and revise their ideas as they progress through the text. Also, it engages them in social interaction (Borasi and Siegel 1990; Borasi et al. 1998).

Students feel a sense of ownership of the text as they monitor their own reading and reflect and revise their ideas as they progress through the text.

"Cloning an author" involves each student in first recording important ideas and ideas that are not understood on index cards. Next, students arrange their cards in a "map" to show how important ideas are related. Students can then work in groups to explain their maps to one another. Several variations of this procedure are described in the literature. For example, one variation that Borasi and Siegel (1990) mention is grouping the cards into categories and making labels to describe each category. Another example of a variation is given by Borasi and her colleagues (1998). They describe how a teacher asked students to record questions, reactions, and thoughts while reading the text and then to use what they had recorded as a basis for further interaction with the text. One such further interaction involved students in reading their partners' cards, selecting cards that seemed most interesting, and discussing them. With this reading strategy, students clone the author's activities (i.e., selecting and organizing important ideas). This activity helps students realize that texts are "open" for multiple interpretations (Borasi et al. 1998).

Borasi and her colleagues (1998) describe how a teacher asked students to record questions, reactions, and thoughts while reading the text and then to use what they had recorded as a basis for further interaction with the text.

"Sketch-to-sketch" involves students in making drawings to express their interpretations of the text or what they have learned from the text. Going from one medium (text) to another (drawing) encourages students to reflect on what they have read from a different perspective (Borasi et al. 1998). Doing so helps students make further connections and conclusions. Below we present how the Borasi-Siegel synthesis was used in two classrooms.

Participants

The classrooms included a ninth-grade algebra classroom located in a predominately black, rural community with a novice teacher and a graduation exit examination class at a predominately black city high school with an experienced teacher. Both schools were in Alabama and had a high percent of students (more than 75 percent) receiving free or reduced price lunch. Both teachers were devoted to teaching mathematics in ways to help students understand and had a good rapport with their students. The experienced teacher had obtained several small grants to buy resources for her class and wanted to become a national board certified teacher. Both teachers were pleased to integrate the reading activities into their instruction.

The Plan for Implementing the Reading Activities

Teachers read excerpts from books and articles related to reading using Borasi's and Siegel's approach and to reformed mathematics teaching advocated by well-known mathematics education researchers and mathematics professional organizations. We discussed these excerpts during the teachers' planning periods and decided on what students would read.

The city high school teacher made several suggestions. For example, she selected excerpts from *Historical Topics for the Mathematics Classroom* (Hallerberg et al. 1989). In general, we chose readings that aligned with district objectives and had the potential to give students a sense that a variety of groups of people contribute to the development of mathematics. Students were able to realize the connections between their own lives and those of the mathematicians in some of the readings. For example, the readings pertaining to Benjamin Banneker gave details about his personal life and painted him as a significant mathematician by eighteenth-century standards. Students at the rural high school in particular were able to identify with Banneker's humble life on a farm in Maryland. In addition to the reading, we tried to enhance the teaching and learning by integrating calculator activities based on a function approach to algebra, integrating activities advocated by the National Council of Teachers of Mathematics (NCTM; specifically the Illuminations Web site), and discussing the different professional development readings with the teachers.

Findings

Overview

A major theme or pattern that emerged from the data was the idea of a community of mathematicians that valued mathematics and was serious about doing mathematics. This theme was demonstrated in the comments that students recorded on their index cards, students' remarks during whole-class and small-group discussions, and teachers' remarks during whole-class discussions and during informal conversations with team members. Because students were not accustomed to this kind of reading in mathematics, the teachers had to negotiate the readings with students on several occasions. Also, teachers adapted the reading strategies to their particular situations or modified them as they saw fit. The following sections contain examples of such classroom experiences.

> **A major theme or pattern that emerged from the data was the idea of a community of mathematicians that valued mathematics and was serious about doing mathematics.**

Egyptian Mathematics/Early Numeration Systems

In both classrooms, students read the following articles from O'Connor and Robertson (2006): "An Overview of Egyptian Mathematics," "Mathematics in Egyptian Papyri," "Egyptian Numerals," and "Ahmes." In addition, the city high school teacher suggested that students read other articles (La Mar 1989; Mortlock 1989; Heinke 1989).These readings were chosen to connect with the beginning objectives in each class.

The two teachers handled the readings in different ways. The city high school teacher had students write their thoughts on the index cards and then discuss their ideas in small groups. The rural high school teacher preferred to orchestrate a whole-class discussion after students completed the cards. She often asked students to read excerpts aloud. Also, the city high school teacher wrote ten fill-in-the-blank questions pertaining to "Egyptian Numeration System" for students to complete after they read this article. In addition to these questions, we created a seven-item survey for students to complete before and after readings related to early numeration systems and other readings, which included an article about Thomas Fuller, an African slave who had an extraordinary ability to perform complicated calculations mentally, and a summary concerning the historical development of algebra.

Students in both classes used the cards to record how the readings related to their existing knowledge, what they did not know, questions, notes, their likes and dislikes, hypotheses, predictions, and what they found interesting. The following excerpt from the card of Joy[1], a student at the city high school, demonstrates some of these ideas:

Students in both classes used the cards to record how the readings related to their existing knowledge, what they did not know, questions, notes, their likes and dislikes, hypotheses, predictions, and what they found interesting.

> I knew already that Egyptian numerals are inscribed in hiero-glyphic, but I didn't know that it was from the royal mace dating back about 3400 B.C. when Menes united the lower and upper kingdoms of Egypt. I think that the symbols are neat and creative. Who invented Egyptian numerals? What made them think of these symbols?

Most students at the rural high school recorded notes on their cards. These notes tended to be more detailed than the students' notes at the city high school. Several students at the rural high school included pictures of the Egyptian numerals in their notes. For example, one of Jim's cards looked like the illustration in figure 6.1.

The cloning-an-author strategy encouraged students to reflect on the readings. As students reflected, they recorded ideas that they probably would not say aloud in class.

The cloning-an-author strategy encouraged students to reflect on the readings. As students reflected, they recorded ideas that they probably would not say aloud in class. Sara at the city high school wrote this about early Egyptians on one of her cards: "They used funny symbols to

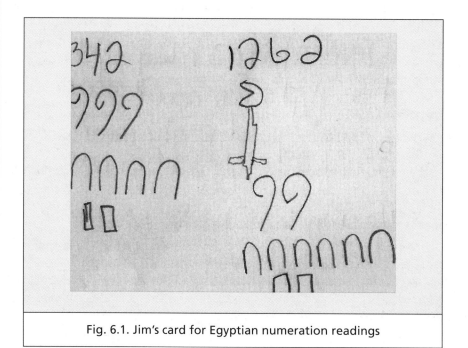

Fig. 6.1. Jim's card for Egyptian numeration readings

---

[1] All students' names are pseudonyms.

represent a number." Some students indicated that they appreciated the early Egyptian numeration system. Sara, for example, wrote on one of her cards, "The Egyptian numeration system have [has] some very wonderful symbols."

Ahmes, Banneker, and False Position

One way that the reading was connected with equations in the rural high school was to allow students to read texts related to the method of false position. The method of false position involves guessing a solution and making a proportional adjustment to find an appropriate one. Thus, to solve $x + x/4 = 15$, one might guess a solution of 4, which gives 5 on the left side of the equation when substituted for x. Noticing that 5 must be multiplied by 3 to get 15 on the right side of the equal sign, one would multiply the initial guess of 4 by 3 to obtain 12, the solution.

Some of the texts discussed Ahmes, an Egyptian scribe who wrote the *Rhind Mathematical Papyrus* and used false position to solve a problem that in modern notation could be given as $x + x/4 = 15$ (O'Connor and Robertson 2006). Other texts were related to Benjamin Banneker, the black American who taught himself how to use the method of false position (Bedini 1999; Mahoney 2004; Mulcrone 1976). Also, for homework, students read an article titled "False Position and Backtracking" (Annenberg Media 2002). A problem to be solved by the method of false position was posed at the end of this article.

The teacher had students use the cloning-an-author approach to read most texts. Most students recorded notes on their index cards. The teacher asked students to read aloud excerpts from *The Life of Benjamin Banneker* (Bedini 1999). She acknowledged and valued students' ideas and did not hesitate to admit that she does not know everything as she orchestrated a discussion about students' index cards for this book. Students showed that they were interested by raising questions and complimenting one another's comments. The following small excerpt from the whole-class discussion demonstrates these ideas:

Teacher:	That's a very important point. Jerry said he wrote down, uh, while he was working on the farm … he would make mathematical puzzles in his mind and try to solve them. What you all think about that? How hard do you all think that must've been? Hmm?
Student:	[inaudible]
Teacher:	To make up your own mathematical puzzles in your mind…. No, I don't think I could…. She [a student] wrote a question [on her index cards]. She asked, "What made Benjamin Banneker so interested in math?" Good question.
Student:	Good question.

> *Teacher:* And, that's what we're going to research. Maybe, eventually, you'll make an *article* where you'll put all the information that we collect together to answer questions. Right now, I honestly, I don't know. I'm learning just like you are. I don't know what made him so interested in math. But, whatever it was, he was very good at it. And we're going to research to learn.... Yeah. We're going to research to learn and read more articles so we can find out what made him so interested in math....

The teacher's comment about writing an article followed up on a suggestion from the research team that students use the texts about Banneker and their index cards to write a paper. Examples follow of comments that students made at the end of their papers about Banneker.

> *Evan:* While reading different articles in class about Banneker I learned many different things about him. I really didn't like it at first, but you have to grow to love certain things.

> *Jim:* What is important about Benjamin Banneker is that he would never quit. Even though he could not continue school, he kept learning. He challenged himself to think up and solve new mathematical problems....

> *Jerry:* I am happy to have had Benjamin Banneker to do a successful critique on. He did miraculous things to spark my heritage and my future.

During the whole-class discussion about the method of false position, the teacher admitted to students that it was confusing to her, but as she talked to the class, she was able to clearly explain what the method involves, compare it with the method she would use, and recognize its importance:

> I personally am having, am still having, a hard time trying to master the whole thought, method, um.... If I saw a problem like what they presented in the article, for example, x plus x over four equal fifteen, ... I would probably solve it by combining like terms and finding the common denominator, whereas he [Ahmes] guessed the answer and then tried to solve from that.... So, I can understand if most of you don't understand how to use it yet.... The more we read about Benjamin Banneker, [the more] it makes me realize how smart he was.... I think what we read about false position ... is important. You all need to take note of that, especially for our exam....

A member of our research team asked the teacher whether she could intervene, and she encouraged students and the teacher to reflect more about the method of false position. She began by asking, "Why did they pick four? You know, they could have picked five, six, seven, eight as a random guess. What was unique about four?" One student said that four simplified the equation. The researcher then created and posed the following equation to students to solve using the method of false position:

One student hypothesized that x would be 6. The researcher plugged 6 into the equation and obtained 2 on the left side. She encouraged students to reflect on the process used in solving the problem that Ahmes solved.

$$x - \frac{2}{3}x = 4$$

Eventually, a student said that the guess of 6 should be multiplied by 2 to obtain 12, the solution. It became clear that the method of false position was "a good cognitive exercise" for students. The teacher indicated that she was now clear about this method, and told the class, "I never heard of false position. So I'm learning just like you are."

The Rectangular Coordinate System

Egyptian coordinate system

Students used the cloning-an-author strategy to read the text related to the Egyptians' use of the coordinate system (Powell and Frankenstein 1997). This text included an architect's drawing dating back to c. 2700 B.C.E. for a section of a temple roof and discussed how the idea of rectangular coordinates was used. An example of the kinds of ideas that students wrote on their cards is given for Sharon. As with the cards for the Egyptian numeration system, false position, and Banneker, students used them to record such things as notes and questions, as well as what they found important or interesting.

> **Contents of Sharon's Card**
> What is an architect's plan on a limestone ostracon?
> What does it mean when it say[s] 1 cubit apart?
> This architect's plan shows the earliest known use of rectangular coordinates. Clarke and Engelbach recognized the architect's plan as being "of great importance."

The rural teacher found this text difficult to understand, even after a research team member tried to clarify it with her. She admitted this difficulty to the students during the whole-class discussion and said that she thought the main purpose was to show that coordinates were used a long time ago by the Egyptians. Students' questions—for example, the meaning of *ostracon*—made it necessary to find Internet resources that gave more background related to the Egyptians' use of the coordinate system.

The rural teacher agreed to allow two pairs of students, Evan and Vivian and Pat and Dan, to record their thoughts about the Egyptian coordinate system using PowerPoint instead of index cards. Pat and Vivian had some prior experience using PowerPoint and were able to guide their partners. The students "decorated" their cards using colorful, patterned backgrounds and word art. They raised several questions (e.g., What does a horizontal coordinate equivalent to 98 fingers mean?) on their PowerPoint slides.

René Descartes

As noted, the rural high teacher was leery about students' using the say-something strategy. In an interview with a member of our research team, she said that she thought that students would respond better to the cloning-an-author strategy because they were "independent workers." However, she agreed that students could use the say-something strategy to read about Descartes, thus connecting with their objective on graphing in two-dimensional space. The teacher explained the say-something strategy to students, summarizing that students needed to discuss the material as they read. She also asked students to write on the index cards if they wished as they used the say-something strategy, and gave them the option of doing their report about either Descartes or Banneker. Interestingly, in the same interview, the teacher indicated that reading in pairs (using the say-something strategy) was pivotal because she thought that students' reading levels were low. Another interesting outcome was that students indicated in an end-semester interview that they liked the say-something strategy. They said that this strategy gave them a chance to understand what others were thinking and to exchange ideas.

Two students, Evan and Dan, used the computer to read an article about Descartes (O'Connor and Robertson 2006). The rest of the class read an excerpt from a text by Rouse Ball (1908), which was a link in the Descartes article. One idea was to encourage discussion about Descartes from the perspectives of two different texts. Evan and Dan would lead the discussion from the perspective of the O'Connor and Robertson text, and the other students would lead the discussion from the perspective of the Ball text. The hope was that Evan and Dan would inquire about and explore other Web-based resources pertaining to Descartes and his mathematical endeavors. Instead, however, Evan and Dan took turns reading aloud and recorded passages verbatim on index cards. They did not seem to reflect on what they were reading. Clearly, Evan and Dan needed guidance on reading reflectively, engaging in dialogue with each other to make sense of the text, and taking advantage of the links included in the Web site that they were reading. Victoria and Ron, who read from the Ball text at their desks, seemed to take advantage of the ideas behind the say-something strategy even before our intervention. They raised questions and explained. Below are some excerpts from their dialogue.

Victoria and Ron (at their desks)

Ron: Stop.

Victoria: What question did you have?

Ron:	When did he die?
Victoria:	He died February 11, 1650.
	...
Victoria:	OK. What do you think about, um, Descartes' character? What kind of person do you think he ...?
Ron:	Famous.
Victoria:	Besides a famous person, like his feelings about mathematics or what did he think?
Ron:	(inaudible) Oh, in the morning before ...
Victoria:	I think he was a very devoted person to mathematics.

Conclusion

Informal comments and formal responses during interviews from teachers and students indicated that they liked reading under the Borasi-Siegel framework. For example, in an interview the rural teacher expressed that the process positively affected her instruction and that the important decisions for the teacher are in choosing readings that will work best for her students. She stated that the important characteristics or hallmarks of the reading experiences done in her class were the index cards and the say-something strategy, because the reading levels were poor in her class.

In another example, one of the students at the rural high school recorded the following in her journal: "What I like about the readings is that each of the reading[s] tells me about *[what] each of the mathematicians went through.*" Possibly this student was beginning to recognize the humanistic side of mathematics!

From our observations we found that reading under the Borasi-Siegel framework benefited the classes in the following ways:

1. Students and teachers learned new ideas, including basic ideas. For example, the rural teacher and students learned the names of the parts of a subtraction problem (i.e., *minuend, subtrahend,* and *difference*) as they read about the historical development of algebra. One interesting outcome was that a student at the rural high school asked me during an interview if the *Wall Street Journal* could be read sometimes. When I asked her how she thought of this publication as a reading source, she said that the television commercials made her think that it would have some interesting ideas connected with mathematics.

2. Students communicated in writing and orally. As they communicated, they acted like a community of mathematicians, even complimenting one another on occasions. To the rural teacher's surprise, both she and the students liked using the say-something strategy.

3. Students and teachers developed appreciation for some mathematical ideas. For example, the rural teacher indicated that she would have difficulty writing numbers using the Egyptian numeration system.

4. Opportunities arose for the rural teacher to model that it was acceptable to make revisions in mathematics and not to understand.

5. The idea of collaboration was modeled to students, especially in the rural classroom when we asked the teacher whether a researcher could intervene during the discussion of false position.

6. Students read in an active way.

In summary, reading under the Borasi-Siegel framework can be advantageous for any classroom, especially diverse classrooms such as those discussed in this article, for five reasons: (1) it is a relatively inexpensive yet effective way to promote reform ideas in mathematics teaching and learning; (2) it encourages both conceptual understanding and a well-rounded view of mathematics as a discipline; (3) it encourages students and teachers to collaborate; (4) it is flexible, as shown by the teachers' sometimes modifying the reading strategies to fit their particular situations; and (5) technology can be easily and effectively incorporated.

One lesson that we learned is the importance of being flexible, which Siegel noted in a telephone conversation. School demands are very great. Often, meetings had to be rescheduled and readings had to be altered because of unexpected events. But even if readings are done for a small number of the district objectives, especially those that would be considered the "big ideas" in algebra, they lead to potential benefits for both students and teachers.

REFERENCES

Annenberg Media Learner.org. "Patterns, Functions, and Algebra—Session 6, Part B: False Position and Backtracking." Annenberg Media. www.learner.org/channel/courses/learningmath/algebra/session6/part_b/index.html.

Ball, Walter William Rouse. "Descartes, 1596–1650." In *A Short Account of the History of Mathematics*, 4th ed. London: Macmillan, 1908. www.maths.tcd.ie/pub/HistMath/People/Descartes/RouseBall/RB_Descartes.html.

Bedini, Silvio A. *The Life of Benjamin Banneker.* Rancho Cordova, Calif.: Landmark Enterprises, 1999.

Borasi, Raffaella, and Marjorie Siegel. "Reading to Learn Mathematics: New Connections, New Questions, New Challenges." *For the Learning of Mathematics* 10, no. 3 (1990): 9–16.

———. *Reading Counts: Expanding the Role of Reading in Mathematics Classrooms.* New York: Teachers College Press, 2000.

Borasi, Raffaella, Marjorie Siegel, Judith Fonzi, and Constance F. Smith. "Using Transactional Reading Strategies to Support Sense-Making and Discussion in Mathematics Classrooms: An Exploratory Study." *Journal for Research in Mathematics Education* 29, no. 3 (May 1998): 275–305.

Hallerberg, Arthur E., John K. Baumgart, Duane E. Deal, and Bruce R. Vogeli, eds. *Historical Topics for the Mathematics Classroom.* Reston, Va.: National Council of Teachers of Mathematics, 1989.

Harste, Jerome C., Kathryn Mitchell Pierce, and Trevor H. Cairney, eds. *The Authoring Cycle: A Viewing Guide.* Portsmouth, N.H.: Heinemann, 1985.

Heinke, Clarence H. "Origins of Symbols for Operations." In *Historical Topics for the Mathematics Classroom,* edited by Arthur E. Hallerberg, John K. Baumgart, Duane E. Deal, and Bruce R. Vogeli, pp. 139–40. Reston, Va.: National Council of Teachers of Mathematics, 1989.

La Mar, Diana. "Egyptian Numeration System." In *Historical Topics for the Mathematics Classroom,* edited by Arthur E. Hallerberg, John K. Baumgart, Duane E. Deal, and Bruce R. Vogeli, pp. 38–40. Reston, Va.: National Council of Teachers of Mathematics, 1989.

Mahoney, John F. "Benjamin Banneker and the Method of Single Position." *Mathematics Teaching in the Middle School* 9, no. 7 (2004): 368–70.

Mortlock, R[oland] S. "Finger Reckoning." In *Historical Topics for the Mathematics Classroom,* edited by Arthur E. Hallerberg, John K. Baumgart, Duane E. Deal, and Bruce R. Vogeli, pp. 120–23. Reston, Va.: National Council of Teachers of Mathematics, 1989.

Mulcrone, Thomas F. "Benjamin Banneker, Pioneer Negro Mathematician." *Mathematics Teacher* 69, no. 2 (February 1976): 155–60.

O'Connor, John J., and Edmund F. Robertson. "The MacTutor History of Mathematics Archive." School of Mathematics and Statistics, University of Saint Andrew, Scotland. www-history.mcs.st-andrews.ac.uk/history/index.html.

Powell, Arthur B., and Marilyn Frankenstein, eds. *Ethnomathematics—Challenging Eurocentrism in Mathematics Education.* Albany: State University of New York Press, 1997.

Rosenblatt, Louise M. *Literature as Exploration.* New York: Appleton-Century, 1938.

———. *The Reader, the Text, the Poem: The Transactional Theory of the Literary Work.* Carbondale: Southern Illinois University Press, 1978.

Siegel, Marjorie, and Raffaella Borasi. "Toward a New Integration of Reading in Mathematics Instruction." *FOCUS on Learning Problems in Mathematics* 14, no. 2 (1992): 18–36.

Siegel, Marjorie, Raffaella Borasi, and Constance F. Smith, C. "A Critical Review of Reading in Mathematics Instruction: The Need for a New Synthesis." In *Cognitive and Social Perspectives for Literacy Research and Instruction,* Thirty-eighth Yearbook of the National Reading Conference, edited by Sandra McCormick and Jerry Zutell, pp. 260–77. Chicago: National Reading Conference, 1989.

7

Generating Problems, Conjectures, and Theorems with Interactive Geometry: An Environment for Fostering Mathematical Thinking by All Students

José N. Contreras

ONE of the goals of mathematics education is to enhance all students' mathematical thinking (National Council of Teachers of Mathematics [NCTM] 2000). To foster their mathematical thinking, students need to be engaged in doing mathematics. Doing mathematics, of course, involves more than performing computations. It entails developing concepts, creating definitions, formulating axioms, deriving formulas, devising algorithms, and developing proofs. These activities are integral parts of doing mathematics. But the heart—the essence—of doing mathematics is posing and solving problems (Contreras 2005; Halmos 1980). As stated by Eves (1981), "the continual appearance of unsolved problems constitutes the life blood that maintains the health and growth of mathematics" (p. 11). Of course, we teachers and teacher educators may not expect students to pose original problems whose solutions will expand the frontiers of mathematical knowledge. What I and other mathematicians, mathematics educators, and professional organizations are advocating is that doing mathematics in classrooms should mirror, to some extent, doing mathematics in the real world: posing and solving problems. One type of common mathematical problem involves developing a proof for a theorem. Once we have solved the proof problem (that is, formulated a theorem), we can modify other attributes of the original problem to pose additional problems that, in turn, give rise to new conjectures and theorems.

The purpose of this article is threefold. First, I describe a framework or model that I have found very useful in helping my students (prospective elementary and secondary school mathematics teachers) learn to generate mathematical problems *systematically*. Second, I describe how I used the model and The Geometer's Sketchpad (GSP) to engage a group of prospective secondary school mathematics teachers (henceforth referred to as students) in creating problems, conjectures, and theorems. The starting mathematical problem was one that is a rich source of appropriate mathematical investigations for high school geometry. The model provided useful strategies to generate worthwhile mathematical problems, whereas the GSP served as a powerful tool to generate and test plausible conjectures. To facilitate the investigation, I provided students with custom tools to expedite the construction of geometric figures, because our focus was on generating

> What I and other mathematicians, mathematics educators, and professional organizations are advocating is that doing mathematics in classrooms should mirror, to some extent, doing mathematics in the real world: posing and solving problems.

problems, conjectures, and theorems rather than on the mechanics of constructing diagrams. The formulation of theorems was supported by proofs validated by students themselves. Most of the proofs involved previously discussed elementary geometric theorems. Third, since many classrooms are diverse in students' learning styles, ability levels, and mathematical backgrounds, I offer some pedagogical tips on how aspects of the investigation can be adapted or differentiated to meet the needs of such students.

The investigation was conducted with seven students enrolled in a required college geometry class. Each student had access to a computer. The investigation described here lasted about two class periods of seventy-five minutes each. The students had extensive experience developing proofs in the contexts of properties of quadrilaterals and circles using congruence and similarity of triangles. Following the customary format of presenting mathematical proofs in mathematics textbooks and journals, I required them to write proofs in narrative form right from the beginning of the semester.

Some Prototypical Problem-Posing Strategies: A Problem-Posing Framework

Given a mathematical problem, we can generate new mathematical problems by modifying some of its attributes. Although different problems have different attributes, a close examination of the different problems that can be generated from a given problem reveals the existence of some archetypical types of mathematical problems: proof problems, converse problems, special problems, general problems, and extended problems (see fig. 7.1). This observation is not surprising, because proving, reversing, specializing, generalizing, and extending are fundamental mathematical processes.

As displayed in the framework, any generated new problem may become a base problem (i.e., a source of additional problems), and, therefore, creating problems may become a never-ending process.

Although different problems have different attributes, a close examination of the different problems that can be generated from a given problem reveals the existence of some archetypical types of mathematical problems: proof problems, converse problems, special problems, general problems, and extended problems.

Starting Our Investigation: Generating Proof Problems

We started our investigation with the following special version of the Varignon problem: Let *ABCD* be a parallelogram and *E, F, G,* and *H* be the midpoints of its consecutive sides. What type of quadrilateral is *EFGH*? (I will refer to *EFGH* as the *medial quadrilateral*. The Varignon parallelogram theorem states that the medial quadrilateral of any quadrilateral is a parallelogram.) As indicated in the framework, a prototypical problem-posing strategy is proving. Proving is an essential component of doing mathematics. It is the mechanism through which mathematical truths are established. From an educational point of view, proving is also an essential pedagogical activity because a proof often reveals or explains why a theorem is true by making more explicit the interconnections of mathematical ideas or principles. Therefore, when dealing with a mathematical problem in open form (e.g., if *E, F, G,* and *H* are the midpoints of the consecutive

Proving is an essential component of doing mathematics.

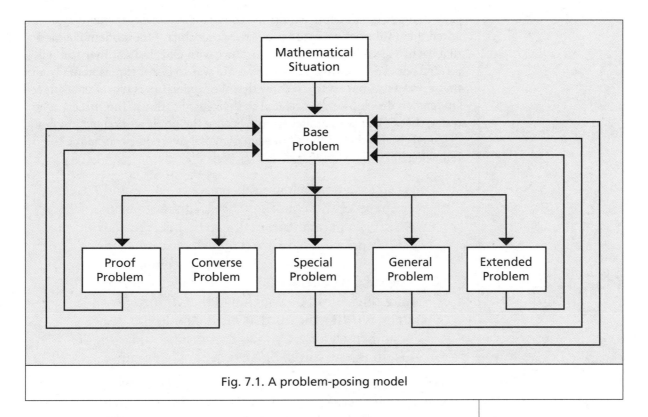

Fig. 7.1. A problem-posing model

sides of parallelogram *ABCD*, what type of quadrilateral is *EFGH?*), a worthwhile task is to reformulate it as a proof problem. Notice, however, that reformulating an open problem as a proof problem requires more than changing the syntactic form of a problem: It demands that the solver know or develop the appropriate supporting evidence, usually a proof.

With the custom tools provided, students quickly generated figure 7.2, without the diagonals and their point of intersection. All students conjectured that quadrilateral *EFGH* is a parallelogram. To test their conjecture, students dragged flexible points of *ABCD* and supplied appropriate measurements. Some students argued that *EFGH* is a parallelogram because it is a quadrilateral with opposite congruent sides. Other students justified the conjecture by verifying that the opposite angles are congruent. Only one student verified that *EFGH* is a parallelogram because the consecutive angles are supplementary, which means that the opposite sides of *EFGH* are parallel. This student also confirmed that the diagonals of *EFGH* bisect

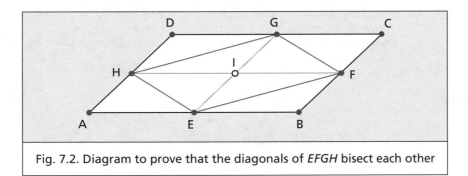

Fig. 7.2. Diagram to prove that the diagonals of *EFGH* bisect each other

each other. After students confirmed their conjecture experimentally, I asked them whether we could prove the conjecture. One student claimed that we had already proved our conjecture with GSP, but another student refuted her claim, stating that what we did was to test it experimentally and that a proof was necessary to show that the conjecture is true. I challenged students to develop a proof related to their justifications. The student who tested that *EFGH* is a parallelogram because the point of intersection of its diagonals is also the midpoint of each diagonal offered a proof along the following lines (fig. 7.2):

> *AEGD* is a parallelogram because sides *AE* and *DG* are parallel and congruent. By a similar reason, *ABFH* is a parallelogram. It can be inferred that *AEIH* and *DGIH* are also parallelograms because their opposite sides are parallel. Since the opposite sides of a parallelogram are congruent and *H* is a midpoint, it can be concluded that *EI = AH = HD = IG*. This means that *I* is the midpoint of *EG*. A similar argument shows that *I* is the midpoint of *FH*. In other words, *EFGH* is a parallelogram.

I was pleased with the variety of strategies that students used to prove their conjecture. As mathematicians often do, after establishing the truth of a conjecture, I asked students to reformulate the initial (base) problem as a proof problem. One student stated the problem as follows:

> Let *ABCD* be a parallelogram and *E, F, G,* and *H* be the midpoints of its consecutive sides. Prove that *EFGH* is a parallelogram. (Problem 1)

Students also reformulated the corresponding conjecture as a theorem. I then asked my students to modify the attributes of the original problem to generate new problems. Since after some time students were still unsure of what I "wanted," I discussed each type of problem included in the problem-posing framework. I then asked them to underline the attributes of the problem that could be changed and then list under each attribute possible changes. Students produced the diagram presented in figure 7.3. Students

Rectangle Rhombus Square Trapezoid Isosceles trapezoid Kite Quadrilateral	Trisection points Four-section points Five-section points	Opposite	Diagonals Interior angles Exterior angles

Fig. 7.3. Potential variations of our base problem

then generated new problems by considering variations of the attribute "parallelogram" because it is the attribute that has special, general, and extended cases, as previously discussed in class. I distributed the types of quadrilaterals among students, making sure that each student could generate a special problem, a general problem, and an extended problem. We first investigated special problems.

Generating Special Problems, Conjectures, and Theorems

As illustrated in the framework, another typical problem-posing strategy is specialization. Specializing is another crucial means to discover mathematical knowledge. A special case may have additional or stronger properties than the original case. Therefore, a special problem is a potentially productive problem to pursue. A special problem is generated when a mathematical object or attribute of a problem is substituted by a particular example or case of the original mathematical object or attribute. About half the group investigated the case when *ABCD* is a rectangle while the other half investigated the case when *ABCD* is a rhombus. Some students formulated their special problems as follows:

> *E, F, G,* and *H* are the midpoints of the sides of a rectangle. What type of quadrilateral is *EFGH*? (Problem 2)

> What type of quadrilateral is formed when the midpoints of the sides of a rhombus are joined? (Problem 3)

I asked students to make a conjecture about the nature of quadrilateral *EFGH* in each case without using GSP. A couple of students argued that the medial quadrilateral in each case is a parallelogram because we had already proved that *EFGH* is a parallelogram regardless of what type of parallelogram *ABCD* is. I was happy when another student said that we already knew that *EFGH* is a parallelogram, but that it may be a special one because *ABCD* is now a special parallelogram. Another student, reasoning by "analogy," claimed that *EFGH* is a rectangle when *ABCD* is a rectangle and a rhombus when *ABCD* is a rhombus. He was surprised when, after dragging a flexible point of the original parallelogram to transform it into a rectangle, he discovered that his conjecture was false. Since students knew that precision is important in making and testing conjectures, most of them *constructed*, using the custom tools, the corresponding diagrams (figs. 7.4 and 7.5). As expected, in each case the parallelogram *EFGH* is indeed a special parallelogram. After students used GSP to conjecture that *EFGH* is a rhombus when *ABCD* is a rectangle and that *EFGH* is a rectangle when *ABCD* is a rhombus, they were asked to prove their assertions. Although all students were able to prove that the medial quadrilateral of a rectangle is a rhombus, only one student proved that the medial quadrilateral of a rhombus is a rectangle.

Specializing is another crucial means to discover mathematical knowledge. A special case may have additional or stronger properties than the original case. Therefore, a special problem is a potentially productive problem to pursue.

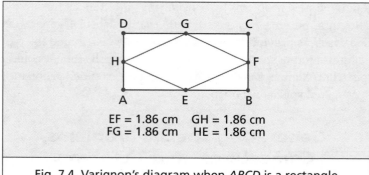

EF = 1.86 cm   GH = 1.86 cm
FG = 1.86 cm   HE = 1.86 cm

Fig. 7.4. Varignon's diagram when *ABCD* is a rectangle

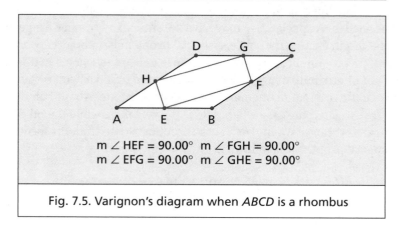

m ∠ HEF = 90.00°   m ∠ FGH = 90.00°
m ∠ EFG = 90.00°   m ∠ GHE = 90.00°

Fig. 7.5. Varignon's diagram when *ABCD* is a rhombus

After having proved their conjectures, students reformulated their problems as proof problems and their conjectures as theorems. I emphasized, again, that one of the mathematical goals of examining a special case is to discover whether the special case has additional or stronger properties. Most students seemed to be excited that in this particular situation, that outcome was indeed true. At this point, I asked students to generate the corresponding problem for a square *ABCD*. A student stated the problem in the following terms: Prove that the medial quadrilateral of a square is a square (Problem 4). Although some students constructed a completed proof from scratch, one student made the following argument:

> Since *ABCD* is a rectangle, we know that *EFGH* is a rhombus. *EFGH* is also a rectangle because *ABCD* is a rhombus. Since *EFGH* is both a rhombus and a rectangle, we know that *EFGH* is a square.

Our next task was to examine general cases of a parallelogram, in other words, quadrilaterals for which a parallelogram is a special case.

Generating General Problems, Conjectures, and Theorems

Another archetypical problem-posing strategy is generalization. Generalization is another vital strategy for enlarging mathematical knowledge. In many instances the same relationship holds for the general case, whereas in others a weaker or more subtle relationship exists; and, of course, in other instances no relationship exists at all. But mathematicians, as insatiable searchers of mathematical patterns and relationships, generalize known problems not only to give rise to a host of new problems but in many situations to develop more general and abstract mathematical concepts, procedures, theorems, or proofs. Hence, a general problem is a worthwhile problem to investigate. A general problem is generated when a mathematical object or attribute of a problem is substituted by another mathematical object or attribute that has as a special case the original object or attribute.

Since a trapezoid was defined as a quadrilateral with at least one pair of parallel sides, students knew that, according to this definition, a parallelogram is a special case of a trapezoid (fig. 7.6). Equivalently, we can say that a trapezoid is a general case of a parallelogram. Similarly, a quadrilateral is a general case of a parallelogram. Again, about half of the students investigated the geometric situation in which *ABCD* is a trapezoid and half of them, the situation in which *ABCD* is an arbitrary quadrilateral. Some students formulated the problems to investigate as follows:

What type of quadrilateral is formed by the midpoints of the sides of a trapezoid? (Problem 5)

ABCD is a general quadrilateral, and *E, F, G,* and *H* are the midpoints of its sides. Is *EFGH* a special quadrilateral? Justify your response. (Problem 6)

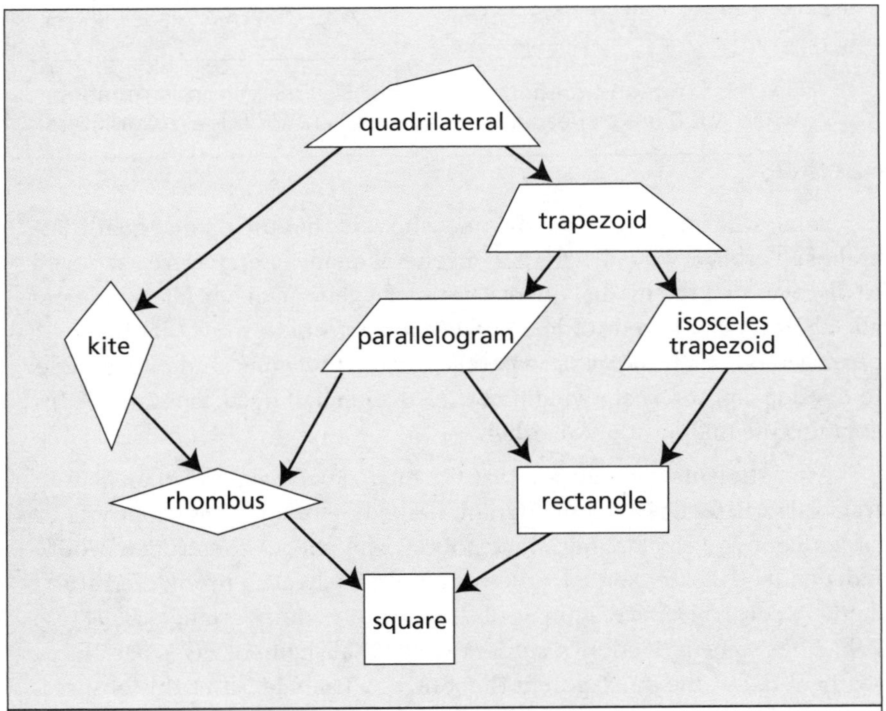

Generalization is another vital strategy for enlarging mathematical knowledge. In many instances the same relationship holds for the general case, whereas in others a weaker or more subtle relationship exists; and, of course, in other instances no relationship exists at all.

Fig. 7.6. A hierarchy of special quadrilaterals

As we can see, the first problem is not well posed in the sense that the midpoints do not form a quadrilateral. I mentioned this issue in class, and a student reformulated the problem in the following terms: What type of quadrilateral is formed when the midpoints of the sides of a trapezoid are joined? (Problem 5b). I asked students to predict the type of medial quadrilateral in each of these two instances without using GSP. One student said that the "inside" quadrilateral for a trapezoid may be a trapezoid or an isosceles trapezoid, whereas another student stated that the inside quadrilateral may also be a parallelogram. Guesses for the medial quadrilateral of an arbitrary quadrilateral included a general quadrilateral, a trapezoid, or a parallelogram. One student said that such a quadrilateral may be a rectangle. Another student refuted this last conjecture by explaining that it cannot be a rectangle because we already know that the medial quadrilateral of a (generic) parallelogram is a parallelogram. After having formulated the problems and making some guesses about the nature of the medial quadrilaterals, students generated the corresponding conjectures using GSP. Figures 7.7 and 7.8 display the diagrams for each problem situation.

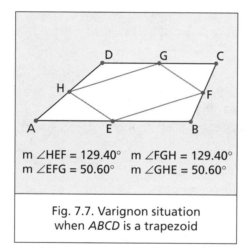

$m \angle HEF = 129.40°$ $m \angle FGH = 129.40°$
$m \angle EFG = 50.60°$ $m \angle GHE = 50.60°$

Fig. 7.7. Varignon situation when *ABCD* is a trapezoid

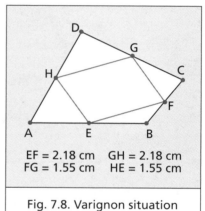

EF = 2.18 cm   GH = 2.18 cm
FG = 1.55 cm   HE = 1.55 cm

Fig. 7.8. Varignon situation when *ABCD* is a quadrilateral

Some students, including the one who said that the medial quadrilateral of an arbitrary quadrilateral is a general quadrilateral, were surprised to discover that the medial quadrilateral of a generic quadrilateral is a parallelogram. I first asked students to develop a proof to show that the medial quadrilateral of a trapezoid is a parallelogram. Only one student was able to develop a proof by showing that each diagonal of quadrilateral *EFGH* contains the midpoint of the other.

After students conjectured that the medial quadrilateral of an arbitrary quadrilateral is a parallelogram, I asked them to develop a proof. This assignment was challenging, since nobody was able to construct a proof independently. After some fruitless attempts to create a proof, I led students to construct the diagonals of *ABCD* and examine triangle *BCD* (fig. 7.9). After some reflection, a student stated that segment *FG* is parallel to segment *BD* by the midsegment theorem of a triangle. After this observation, similar conclusions were reached by other students regarding the other sides of quadrilateral *EFGH*. After justifying that the opposite sides of *EFGH* are parallel, students concluded that *EFGH* is a parallelogram regardless of what type of quadrilateral *ABCD* is. After having constructed the proofs, students reformulated their original general problems as proof problems. I emphasized that we had not only generalized the theorem but also found a more general proof that shows that the medial quadrilateral of any quadrilateral is a parallelogram.

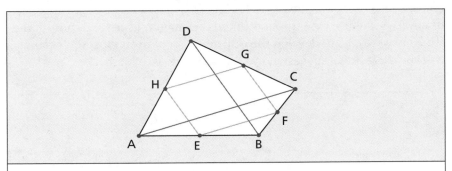

Fig. 7.9. Diagram to prove that *EFGH* is a parallelogram when *ABCD* is a quadrilateral

Our next task was to extend our base problem to kites and isosceles trapezoids.

Generating Extended Problems, Conjectures, and Theorems

As the framework shows, another common strategy to generate problems is extension. Extending mathematical relationships and concepts is another common means of generating mathematical knowledge. Consequently, an extended problem may be a fruitful problem to solve. An extended problem is created when a mathematical object or attribute of a problem is substituted by another similar or analogous mathematical object or attribute. In this instance, neither of the involved mathematical objects is a special case of the other. Since an isosceles trapezoid and a kite are not special cases of a parallelogram and vice versa (fig. 7.6), we can say that the problem is extended to other cases.

At this point, having proved that the medial quadrilateral of an arbitrary quadrilateral *ABCD* is always a parallelogram, we seem to have little to discover about the medial quadrilateral of either an isosceles trapezoid or a kite. But, as one of the students remarked, the medial quadrilateral of an isosceles trapezoid or a kite may be a special parallelogram because an isosceles trapezoid and a kite are special quadrilaterals. To continue our investigation, some students generated an extended problem for a kite and others, for an isosceles trapezoid. Two students formulated their extended problems as follows:

> If *ABCD* is an isosceles trapezoid and *E, F, G,* and *H* are the midpoints of its sides, prove that *EFGH* is a rhombus. (Problem 7)

Extending mathematical relationships and concepts is another common means of generating mathematical knowledge.

What type of quadrilateral is the medial quadrilateral of a kite? (Problem 8)

The student who formulated the first of these problems did not use GSP to generate her problem because, as she said, the proof is straightforward. However, for the other students, the use of GSP was instrumental to test their respective conjectures for several isosceles trapezoids and types of kites, including nonconvex kites. Figures 7.10 and 7.11 display their discoveries. Some of the students found the results surprising. Most of the students were able to develop the respective proof to support their claims that the conjectures suggested by GSP were actual theorems.

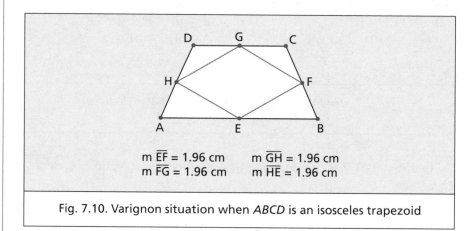

m $\overline{EF}$ = 1.96 cm   m $\overline{GH}$ = 1.96 cm
m $\overline{FG}$ = 1.96 cm   m $\overline{HE}$ = 1.96 cm

Fig. 7.10. Varignon situation when *ABCD* is an isosceles trapezoid

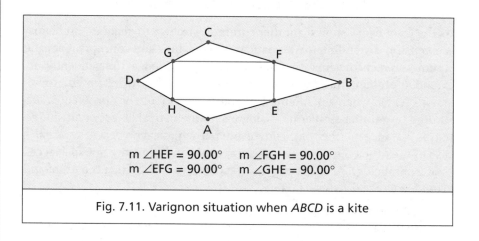

m $\angle HEF$ = 90.00°   m $\angle FGH$ = 90.00°
m $\angle EFG$ = 90.00°   m $\angle GHE$ = 90.00°

Fig. 7.11. Varignon situation when *ABCD* is a kite

To continue our investigation, we summarized our findings in a table (see table 7.1). We then investigated converse problems as well as problems involving different types of *n*-section points. The students also investigated area and perimeter relationships between quadrilaterals and inner quadrilaterals for a diversity of *n*-section points. Our original problem was indeed a rich source of problems, conjectures, and theorems.

Table 7.1
Relationship between Quadrilateral ABCD *and Its Medial Quadrilateral* EFGH

Quadrilateral *ABCD*	Quadrilateral *EFGH*
1. Parallelogram	Parallelogram
2. Rectangle	Rhombus
3. Rhombus	Rectangle
4. Square	Square
5. Isosceles trapezoid	Rhombus
6. Kite	Rectangle
7. Trapezoid	Parallelogram
8. Quadrilateral	Parallelogram

Reflections on Adapting and Differentiating the Investigation for a Diverse Group of Students

This investigation could be adapted for high school students with a diversity of backgrounds. In this section I describe some pedagogical tips that teachers may find helpful when adapting or differentiating aspects of this investigation to meet the needs of groups of students having a diversity of learning styles, cognitive ability, and mathematical background. I focus my discussion on the three main components of the investigation: generating problems, creating conjectures, and formulating theorems. Research and my own experience suggest that even though students have some natural abilities to generate problems, their problems tend to be trivial, random, and in many instances unproductive to pursue (Knuth 2002). Since my own experiences had suggested that students do not systematically and consistently apply the fundamental processes of proving, reversing, specializing, generalizing, and extending to generate problems, I developed the problem-posing framework displayed in figure 7.1. I have found this framework to be a powerful guide to enhance my own (Contreras 2003) and my students' abilities to pose worthwhile geometric problems.

However, generating these types of problems can be a challenge for some students. To overcome some of the difficulties, students need to have previous experiences in distinguishing among special, extended, and general cases of a specific mathematical object—in this instance, of special quadrilaterals. The hierarchy of quadrilaterals (fig. 7.6) was for most of my students a helpful visual representation of the relationship among the different types of quadrilaterals. Still, a student needed to see the hierarchy constantly to visualize such relationships. Thus, especially for those who

By engaging students in problem generation with the aid of the problem-posing model, we can give more students access to doing mathematics than with the traditional approach.

need a visual representation, the hierarchy is important to have available when generating special, general, and extended problems. Unquestionably, the framework was a useful tool that enabled *all* students to formulate worthwhile mathematical problems. It played an important role in indicating the nature of the problems that my students generated and pursued. By engaging students in problem generation with the aid of the problem-posing model, we can give more students access to doing mathematics than with the traditional approach.

GSP was instrumental not only in testing the conjectures but also in students' own problem generation, two important aspects of doing mathematics. To justify their conjectures, students used the measurement capabilities of GSP. For example, to justify that the medial quadrilateral of a rectangle is a rhombus (fig. 7.4), students used GSP to confirm that all the sides of *EFGH* are congruent, suggesting that *EFGH* is a rhombus. A common issue is that some students may apply the framework in a mechanical and mindless way. To decrease the likelihood of their doing so, students need to reflect on the potential problems and use GSP to verify the plausibility of the corresponding conjectures. In some instances, GSP also helped my students reformulate an ill-posed problem as a well-posed problem (e.g., reformulating the problem "prove that the medial quadrilateral of a rectangle is a rectangle" as "prove that the medial quadrilateral of a rectangle is a rhombus"). From this perspective, GSP played a primordial role in the final formulation of many problems and the generation of the corresponding conjectures. Undeniably, I can say that GSP was a powerful pedagogical environment that supported *all* students in their conjecture-generation endeavors. By engaging students in the process of generating and justifying conjectures with GSP, more students can be involved in doing mathematics than with the traditional approach.

The generation of theorems was a more challenging task, since it was required that a conjecture could be ascended to the rank of theorem only if we could prove it. Making students' arguments public helped them refute and validate their explanations and justifications. In some instances, I needed to provide them with a "hint" so we could progress in our investigations. All these factors, students' refutations and validations as well as my hints, helped all my students in their constructions of mathematical proofs to support their theorems. The argument could be made that college mathematics students are more mature mathematically than high school students and that some of the proofs may not be appropriate for all high school students. Under these constraints, the teacher may need to provide more guidance and hints to help *all* students develop or understand some of the proofs.

One of the strengths of the investigation is that it generates theorems whose proofs vary in levels of difficulty. This aspect allows more students to have experiences in constructing mathematical arguments. Still, teachers can further differentiate the level of justification to meet the needs of more students, if needed. At the next lower level, students can use numerical data to justify a specific case. For example, to justify that the medial quadrilateral of a rhombus is a rectangle (fig. 7.5), students can be given the measure of an interior angle of a rhombus, say *A*, to obtain, by justifying the process, the measures of the interior angles of quadrilateral *EFGH*. At the very minimum, students can use GSP to provide empirical evidence to justify their conjectures, as described above. By being allowed a variety of justifications, more students get access to doing mathematics than with the traditional approach.

Conclusion

Students need to have the appropriate mathematical and GSP background when performing open investigations like the one described in this article. My students were familiar with the hierarchy of quadrilaterals and the notions of special, general, and extended cases among quadrilaterals. They were also already familiar with all the GSP features that they used in the investigation. In addition, my students had extensive experience in developing proofs and were also familiar with properties of special quadrilaterals as well as with the theorems needed to construct the proofs. This background was crucial to applying the problem-posing framework to generate worthwhile mathematical problems, use GSP to test the created conjectures, and formulate the theorems by constructing mathematical proofs. By generating problems, conjectures, and theorems, students were engaged in important mathematical processes.

Differentiating instruction by focusing not only on proofs but also on generating problems and formulating and testing conjectures, we can provide access to mathematics and engage more students in doing mathematics than with the traditional approach. In closing, I would like to reiterate that all students should experience the thrill of doing mathematics: generating problems, conjectures, and theorems, even if they are new only to them. These mathematical activities not only foster students' mathematical thinking and creativity but also enrich their view of what constitutes doing mathematics.

REFERENCES

Contreras, José. "A Problem-Posing Approach to Specializing, Generalizing, and Extending Problems with Interactive Geometry Software." *Mathematics Teacher* 96, no. 4 (April 2003): 270–76.

———. "Posing and Solving Problems: The Essence and Legacy of Mathematics." *Teaching Children Mathematics* 12, no. 3 (October 2005): 115–16.

Eves, Howard. *Great Moments in Mathematics (after 1650)*. Washington D.C.: Mathematical Association of America, 1981.

Halmos, Paul R. "The Heart of Mathematics." *American Mathematical Monthly* 87, no. 7 (August-September 1980): 519–24.

Knuth, Eric J. "Fostering Mathematical Curiosity." *Mathematics Teacher* 95, no. 2 (February 2002): 126–30.

National Council of Teachers of Mathematics (NCTM). *Principles and Standards for School Mathematics*. Reston, Va.: NCTM, 2000.

8

Egyptian Fractions, a Graphing Calculator, and Rational Functions: 2000 BC Mathematics with AD 2000 Tools

Armando M. Martinez-Cruz
José N. Contreras

THE HISTORY of mathematics (e.g., Boyer 1968; Dunham 1990; Newman 1956) reveals many instances in which mathematical ideas or problems were approached in antiquity and later revisited by other mathematicians who had access to different mathematical tools. For instance, Archimedes (287–212 BC) estimated the value of π using inscribed and circumscribed polygons to a circle, and about nineteen centuries later, Newton (1642–1726) used more sophisticated mathematical tools (algebra, power series, and calculus) to get a better approximation. Newton was not the only one who worked on this problem. In fact, in this almost-2000-year period, other mathematicians made other estimates for π. Each approach is meritorious, and all of them teach us different ideas. First, we observe how mathematical problems start, have been approached, develop, and become more sophisticated. Second, we see how our ancestors engaged in fascinating mathematical ideas and were able to derive solutions even with limited mathematical tools, as in the example of Archimedes, when computing devices where unthinkable. Third, each approach helps us appreciate and make connections within mathematical ideas. Fourth, sometimes we observe in the classroom that students use the "old approaches" to solve problems—as if history repeats itself while they are learning a concept. Finally, in the specific case of π, we observe changes in the way the estimation was approached. Archimedes used a geometric method, but by Newton's time the problem had become arithmetical

Mathematics teachers today have plenty of opportunities to revisit topics from antiquity with sophisticated pedagogical and mathematical tools. For example, teachers can use graphing calculators and dynamical geometry software to illustrate Newton's and Archimedes' approximations to π. Indeed, "technology is essential in teaching and learning mathematics; it influences the mathematics that is taught and enhances students' learning" (National Council of Teachers of Mathematics [NCTM] 2000, p. 24). One needs only to glance at current mathematics education journals to find ideas on how to incorporate history, mathematics, and technology into the classroom. Recently, Özgün-Koca (2007) discussed how Archimedes' method to approximate π can be employed with technology to teach limits.

Mathematics teachers today have plenty of opportunities to revisit topics from antiquity with sophisticated pedagogical and mathematical tools. For example, teachers can use graphing calculators and dynamical geometry software to illustrate Newton's and Archimedes' approximations to π.

Graphing technology can also provide a nurturing learning environment for all students.

This article has the spirit of recent reform calls in mathematics education to integrate technology in the teaching and learning of mathematics (NCTM 2000). In particular, we address how graphing technology can also provide a nurturing learning environment for all students. Here, we revisit a problem from around 2000 BC—expressing a fraction as the sum of fractions whose numerator is a unit—with more sophisticated tools (rational functions) and twentieth-century graphing technology. Our discussion contains three parts. In the first section, we present a brief comment on arithmetic in ancient Egypt, introduce unit fractions, and demonstrate an arithmetic method for expressing fractions as the sum of unit fractions. In the next section, we use a graphing calculator and properties of a rational function to determine graphically some ways to express a fraction as the sum of two unit fractions. We conclude the article with a method to determine all the ways to express a fraction as the sum of two unit fractions, sketching how to determine some of the ways a fraction can be expressed as the sum of three unit fractions. This last portion suggests that the number of ways a fraction can be expressed as the sum of unit fractions is infinite.

Graphs and tables of rational functions in a graphing calculator are used to illustrate how technology can offer different points of entrance into expressing fractions as a sum of unit fractions. In this way students can still explore mathematical problems using a calculator if the solutions are not accessible to them through other mathematical approaches. We have discussed some of the ideas presented here with preservice elementary and secondary school teachers and with current secondary school teachers. At the end of the article, we suggest when some material can be discussed with students at the high school level. We use a TI-84 in the article, but any graphing calculator with a table feature can be used to follow the discussion.

Arithmetic in Egypt

We learn from papyruses that mathematics was studied in Egypt at least 4000 years ago. Among the papyruses that exist, the Rhind papyrus (after the Englishman A. Henry Rhind, who bought it in 1858) is the best source of information that we have of Egyptian mathematics. Egyptians performed computations, but we can only speculate about how they developed the methods: the Rhind papyrus presents solutions to problems, not the way the answers were found. Egyptians used a decimal system, and could perform basic operations of addition, subtraction, multiplication, and division. However, they approached multiplications by doubling and adding. For instance, to compute 28 times 7, they proceeded as shown in figure 8.1, although with different notation. They also computed divisions by doubling and adding; fractions emerged as the result of not having a remainder zero.

A general fraction was a mystery for the Egyptians; not an elementary entity but "as part of an uncompleted process ... reducible to the sum of unit fractions" (Boyer 1968, pp. 13–14). A unit fraction is a fraction whose

28 times 1 is 28

28 times 2 is 56 (doubled)

28 times 4 is 112 (doubled the previous quantity)

Since 7 = 4 + 2 + 1, we add 28 + 56 + 112 to get 196.

Fig. 8.1. Egyptian computation for 28 times 7

numerator is a unit. Egyptians used them to represent all fractions except 2/3 and 3/4, which were used in arithmetic methods. As we will see next, a fraction can be expressed in many ways as the sum of unit fractions. Two situations about the Egyptian expressions are unclear to us: (1) why one breakdown was preferred over another, and (2) why the repetition of a unit fraction was not allowed. For instance, 1/2 was not expressed as 1/4 + 1/4.

Expressing a Fraction as the Sum of Unit Fractions

Egyptian mathematicians manipulated unit fractions skillfully and solved problems that "the average intelligent man of the modern world" (Newman 1956, p. 171) would have difficulties solving. Some secondary school mathematics teachers struggle when we ask them to express a fraction (say, 3/5) as the sum of unit fractions with no repetition. After some time, some find the solution 3/5 = 1/2 + 1/10, whereas others state the solution 3/5 = 1/2 + 1/12 + 1/60. They typically find the largest unit fraction less than the given fraction. For 3/5, we have 1/2 < 3/5. Next, they compute the difference of these fractions: 3/5 −1/2 = 1/10, and get 3/5 = 1/2 + 1/10. Actually, mathematicians have studied how Egyptians might have expressed fractions as the sum of unit fractions. One of those mathematicians, J. J. Sylvester (1814–1897), proposed the method used by our teachers (Bunt, Jones, and Bedient 1976, p. 17). Sylvester's work not only validates students' own invented method in this instance but also suggests that teachers should encourage students to invent methods as alternative ways to solve problems, and therefore give more students access to mathematics. Bunt, Jones, and Bedient (1976) and Boyer (1968) present tentative ideas on the way Egyptians expressed fractions as the sum of unit fractions on the basis of their basic operations. We encourage readers to consult both references.

The Rhind papyrus contains about eighty mathematical problems. Six of those problems involve dividing loaves of bread among men. We use this sharing of breads to illustrate a visual (and different) way of expressing a fraction as the sum of different unit fractions. Let us think of 3/5 again. We make the problem concrete by thinking that we have three pieces of bread and we want to share them among five people. How can we share the bread so that each person gets the same amount of bread expressed in unit fractions?

Start with three pieces of bread, and divide each piece into two pieces to get six pieces in total. Why six? Six is the first multiple of three larger than five. Give to each person one of these pieces, namely half a loaf of bread (see fig. 8.2).

Some secondary school mathematics teachers struggle when we ask them to express a fraction (say, 3/5) as the sum of unit fractions with no repetition.

Teachers should encourage students to invent methods as alternative ways to solve problems, and therefore give more students access to mathematics.

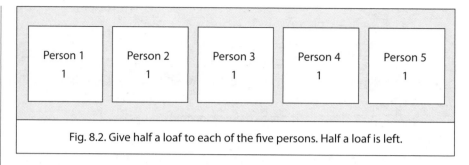

Fig. 8.2. Give half a loaf to each of the five persons. Half a loaf is left.

Next divide the last half-loaf of bread left into five equal pieces, each of them being $1/2 \times 1/5 = 1/10$, and give one to each person. Each person receives $1/2 + 1/10$ as before (see fig. 8.3).

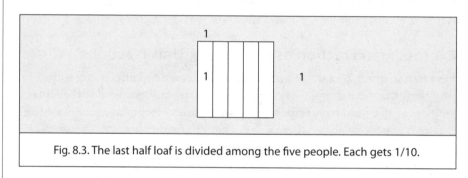

Fig. 8.3. The last half loaf is divided among the five people. Each gets 1/10.

The second solution, namely, $3/5 = 1/2 + 1/12 + 1/60$, results from dividing the three loaves of bread into six pieces (1/2 each) and giving to each of the five persons one of those pieces. Then dividing the half-loaf left into six pieces, each of them being $1/12 = 1/2 \times 1/6$, and give each person one of them, to be left with 1/12. Finally, this last piece is divided into five pieces, each of them being $1/60 = 1/12 \times 1/5$. Again, we do not know why the Egyptians would have preferred one solution over the other. This concrete approach leads to a pedagogical benefit. Students who struggle with manipulating fractions still have access to this content.

Several questions come to mind at this point. First of all, do other ways exist to express 3/5 as the sum of two unit fractions? If so, can we find them all? The next section addresses these two questions. We will use more sophisticated tools, rational functions and a graphing calculator (graphs and tables), to answer these questions. These new tools will make obvious the transition of approaches: An arithmetical approach transitions mainly into a graphical approach.

Do other ways exist to express 3/5 as the sum of two unit fractions? If so, can we find them all?

Rational Functions to Express a Fraction as the Sum of Unit Fractions

We first describe how to express a fraction as the sum of two unit fractions. In a mathematics problem-solving course for secondary school mathematics teachers, we typically work with and discuss unit fractions early in the semester. Last fall, we assigned the following problem as the course approached the end.

A point (x, y) is called integral if both x and y are integers. How many points on the graph of

$$\frac{1}{x} + \frac{1}{y} = \frac{1}{4}$$

are integral points? (Source: "Calendar," Problem 28, November 2006 *Mathematics Teacher*, p. 265)

One teacher while presenting her solution mentioned that she thought this problem looked like it was related to unit fractions. Her comment inspired us to think more in depth about this problem. We realized that when this problem is restricted to positive integer solutions, it provides the ways to express 1/4 as the sum of two unit fractions. To determine the solutions, we graphed the rational function

$$y = \frac{4x}{x - 4},$$

which is obtained from $1/x + 1/y = 1/4$ after solving for y. Since, x and y need to be positive integers in the unit-fraction problem, we needed to study the graph of this function only in the first quadrant. Figure 8.4 shows the graph of this function in the window $(-10, 20) \times (-10, 20)$. We find that the graph of

$$y = \frac{4x}{x - 4}$$

has a vertical asymptote at $x = 4$ by setting the denominator equal to zero, $x - 4 = 0$. Since the graph shows that $y < 0$ when $x = 1, 2, 3$ (see fig. 8.4), we focused only on values when $x > 4$.

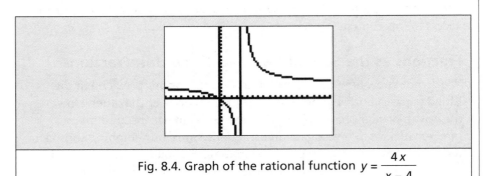

Fig. 8.4. Graph of the rational function $y = \dfrac{4x}{x - 4}$

Next, we used the table capabilities on the TI-84 to evaluate

$$y = \frac{4x}{x - 4}.$$

Figure 8.5 shows the values of

$$y = \frac{4x}{x - 4}$$

for the first twenty-one counting numbers.

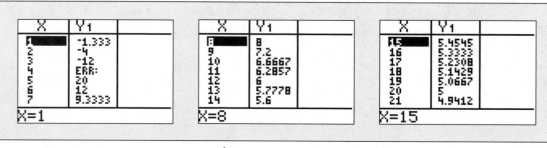

Fig. 8.5. The values of $y = \frac{4x}{x-4}$ for the first twenty-one counting numbers

Since the graph of

$$y = \frac{4x}{x-4}$$

is decreasing in the first quadrant and has a horizontal asymptote at $y = 4$, we knew that once y was less than 5, no more positive integer solutions existed. The tables in figure 8.5 show five solutions: (5, 20), (6, 12), (8, 8), (12, 6), and (20, 5). We disregarded the last two because they give the same solution as the first two. We concluded that we can express 1/4 in three ways as the sum two unit fractions:

$$1/4 = 1/5 + 1/20$$
$$= 1/6 + 1/12$$
$$= 1/8 + 1/8$$

We will use graphs and tables of rational functions to determine all the ways to express 3/5 as the sum of two unit fractions.

We remarked in class again that Egyptians did not repeat fractions. So only two ways can be used to express 1/4 as the sum of unit fractions when history is kept in mind. Before we continue with our discussion, let us mention that this graphical-tabular approach is another avenue to give students access to this content.

Fractions as the Sum of Two and Three Unit Fractions

We do not know how Egyptians found the expressions provided in the Rhind papyrus nor why they used one expression over the other. However, the way they might have approached the problem has inspired many mathematicians to investigate unit fractions. Since our graphing approach was fruitful, we will use graphs and tables of rational functions to determine all the ways to express 3/5 as the sum of two unit fractions. Notice how our question has changed. We are interested now in *all the ways* to express a fraction. We restate first our problem as follows.

Determine all the positive integral solutions to $1/x + 1/y = 3/5$.

First, solve for y in this equation, get the rational function

$$y = \frac{5x}{3x-5},$$

and graph it. Figure 8.6 shows the graph in the window $(-10, 10) \times (-10, 10)$.

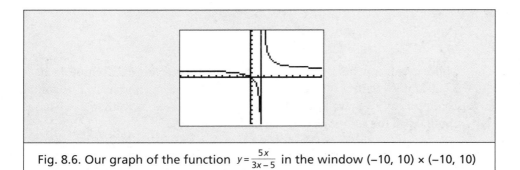

Fig. 8.6. Our graph of the function $y = \frac{5x}{3x-5}$ in the window $(-10, 10) \times (-10, 10)$

The graph of

$$y = \frac{5x}{3x - 5},$$

has a vertical asymptote at $x = 5/3$. From the graph, we notice that we need to focus on the values $x > 1$. Since the graph is decreasing in the first quadrant and has a horizontal asymptote at $y = 5/3$, we notice that once $y < 2$, we have all the solutions. Figure 8.7 shows the tables for $1 < x < 15$. So the only way to express 3/5 as the sum of two unit fractions is 3/5 = 1/2 + 1/10. This is one of the solutions that we found when we shared three loaves of bread among five people.

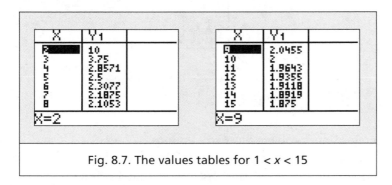

Fig. 8.7. The values tables for $1 < x < 15$

Readers might have noticed that the use of rational functions is quite simple with the availability of graphing technology. Hence students who struggle with algebraic manipulations can have access to this content. We will take it to another level. We are now interested in the following problem.

Find several ways to express 3/5 as the sum of three unit fractions.

Since we know that 3/5 = 1/2 + 1/10 is the only way to express 3/4 as the sum of two unit fractions, we will determine all the ways to express 1/2 and 1/10 each as the sum of two unit fractions. Then we will replace each answer for 1/2, and then for 1/10, in 3/5 = 1/2 + 1/10 to determine other solutions.

First, to determine all the ways to express 1/2 as the sum of two unit fractions, look for the positive integral solutions to $1/x + 1/y = 1/2$. From this expression, we obtain the rational function

$$y = \frac{2x}{x - 2},$$

whose graph appears in figure 8.8. This graph has a vertical asymptote at $x = 2$, and $y = 0$ for $x = 1$. Since the graph is decreasing and has a horizontal asymptote at $y = 2$, we know that once the y-values are less than 3, we have obtained all the solutions (see the table in fig. 8.9).

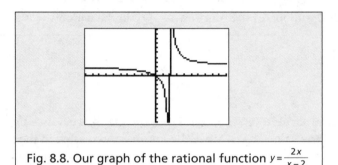

Fig. 8.8. Our graph of the rational function $y = \frac{2x}{x-2}$

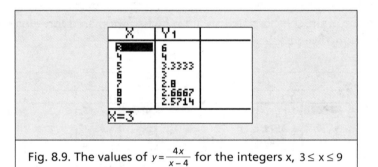

Fig. 8.9. The values of $y = \frac{4x}{x-4}$ for the integers x, $3 \le x \le 9$

Therefore, our problem has two solutions, $1/2 = 1/3 + 1/6$ and $1/2 = 1/4 + 1/4$. But only the first one, $1/2 = 1/3 + 1/6$, would have been used by the Egyptians. In the case of $1/10$, we use the rational function

$$y = \frac{10x}{x - 10},$$

obtained from the problem of determining the positive integral solutions to $1/x + 1/y = 1/10$. The graph of

$$y = \frac{10x}{x - 10}$$

appears in figure 8.10 in the window $(-10, 40) \times (-10, 40)$ with a scale of 5 on both axes.

This graph has a vertical asymptote at $x = 10$, and $y < 0$ for $1 < x < 10$. Since the function is decreasing in the first quadrant and has a horizontal asymptote at $y = 10$, we know that once $y < 11$, we have all the solutions. This result occurs when $x = 111$. Figure 8.11 shows only the tables that contain solutions to the problem. They are (11, 110), (12, 60), (14, 35), (15, 30), (20, 20), (30, 15), (35, 14), (60, 12), and (110, 11).

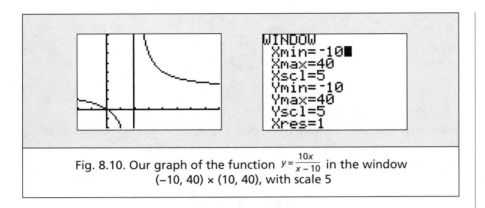

Fig. 8.10. Our graph of the function $y = \frac{10x}{x-10}$ in the window (−10, 40) × (10, 40), with scale 5

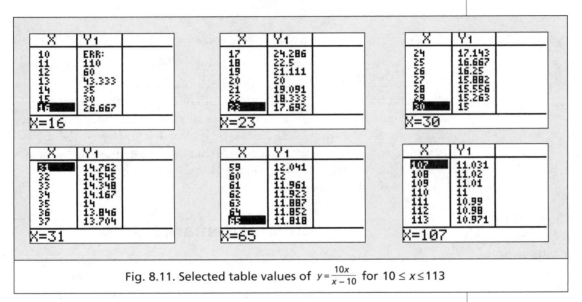

Fig. 8.11. Selected table values of $y = \frac{10x}{x-10}$ for $10 \leq x \leq 113$

All these solutions are plotted in figure 8.12 using the ZoomSquare on the TI-84. One can observe some symmetry in their distribution. Furthermore, the solutions start repeating after we determine the solution that the Egyptians did not accept, namely, (20, 20).

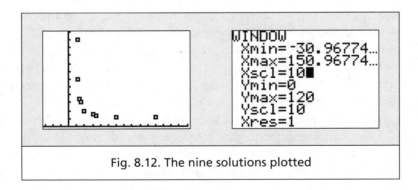

Fig. 8.12. The nine solutions plotted

From the tables, we obtain four solutions to our problem, after eliminating (20, 20):

The fraction 3/5 can be expressed in an infinite way as the sum of unit fractions.

$$1/10 = 1/11 + 1/110$$
$$= 1/12 + 1/60$$
$$= 1/14 + 1/35$$
$$= 1/15 + 1/30$$

Substituting the solutions for 1/2, and then for 1/10, in 3/5 = 1/2 + 1/10, we obtain several ways to express 3/5 as the sum of unit fractions: Using the unique solution 1/2 = 1/3 + 1/6, we obtain one solution: 3/5 = 1/3 + 1/6 + 1/10. Using the four solutions for 1/10, we get four more solutions:

$$3/5 = 1/2 + 1/11 + 1/110$$
$$= 1/2 + 1/12 + 1/60$$
$$= 1/2 + 1/14 + 1/35$$
$$= 1/2 + 1/15 + 1/30$$

Therefore, the fraction 3/5 can be expressed in a unique way as the sum of two unit fractions, but in at least five different ways as the sum of three unit fractions. Continuing this process, we can show that the fraction 3/5 can be expressed in an infinite way as the sum of unit fractions. The same reasoning applies to any fraction. Notice that we do not obtain all ways to express 3/5 as the sum of three unit fractions, since the expression 1/3 + 1/5 + 1/15 is not included here.

Closing Remarks

In this article, we have discussed how rational functions on a graphing calculator can be used to determine the ways to express a fraction as the sum of unit fractions. Egyptians used unit fractions, but we do not know how they determined the expressions. We introduced an arithmetic method to determine some solutions. However, with the use of more sophisticated tools, such as rational functions and readily available graphing technology, we were able to use a graphing approach first and then to determine all the ways to express some fractions as the sum of two unit fractions and several ways to express a fraction as the sum of three unit fractions. Specifically, we used tables and graphs generated by the calculator to investigate and solve the problem. This use of technology addresses the needs of diverse learners. Students who might struggle manipulating fractions or algebraic expression can nevertheless have access to the mathematical ideas presented through graphs and tables. Furthermore, students who have struggled to develop deep understanding of fractions can gain a better understanding of fractional relationships as they proceed through the ideas mentioned in the article. The use of rational functions requires familiarity with basic properties of these functions, such as intervals where they are increasing, vertical and horizontal asymptotes, and domain. Since we are using only basic properties, the approach is quite accessible to second-year algebra students who have access to a graphing calculator. Most high school students would understand the concrete approach of sharing loaves of bread.

Students who might struggle manipulating fractions or algebraic expression can nevertheless have access to the mathematical ideas presented through graphs and tables. Furthermore, students who have struggled to develop deep understanding of fractions can gain a better understanding of fractional relationships as they proceed through the ideas mentioned in the article.

Problems from antiquity can be revisited with current technology. They allow us to learn about ancient methods and integrate mathematics ideas when these problems are approached with current tools. The teacher can introduce students to different strategies and techniques that mathematicians have used to solve the same problem as a way to encourage students to become familiar with those methods and produce their own invented methods. This approach would offer additional access for those students who struggle with methods presented in schools but can use their own strategies or alternative procedures. The spirit of our work is stated by Aristotle (cited in Newman 1956, p. 170), "Here and elsewhere we shall not obtain the best insight into things until we actually see them growing from the beginning."

REFERENCES

Boyer, Carl B. *A History of Mathematics.* New York: John Wiley & Sons, 1968.

Bunt, Lucas N. H., Phillip S. Jones, and Jack D. Bedient. *The Historical Roots of Elementary Mathematics.* New York: Dover, 1976.

"Calendar" [Problem 28]. *Mathematics Teacher* 100, no. 4 (November 2006): 265.

Dunham, William. *Journey through Genius: The Great Theorems of Mathematics.* New York: John Wiley & Sons, 1990.

National Council of Teachers of Mathematics (NCTM). *Principles and Standards for School Mathematics.* Reston, Va.: NCTM, 2000.

Newman, James R. "The Rhind Papyrus." In *The World of Mathematics*, vol. 1, edited by James R. Newman, pp. 170–78. New York: Simon & Schuster, 1956.

Özgün-Koca, S. Asli. "Use of Archimedes' Process for Approximating Circle Area as an Introduction to Limits." *Mathematics Teacher* 100, no. 8 (April 2007): 550–55.

9

Moving from Deficiencies to Possibilities: Some Thoughts on Differentiation in the Mathematics Classroom

Mark W. Ellis

> What the learners conflict with in the mathematics classroom may not only be the mathematical meaning of a particular piece of content or a particular strategy, but the whole act of being taught through processes that ignore, reject or make invisible some students, processes destined to select a few and fail the rest.
>
> —*Núria Gorgorió and Núria Planas*

KATHLEEN Collins' (2003) eighteen-month case study of Jay, a fifth-grade African American student, documents in detail the ways in which those in authority in school "pathologized Jay's family structure, his cultural way of being" (p. 194) such that he was labeled as having low ability and was held to lower expectations by his teacher. Even after Collins shared samples of his work that clearly exhibited cognitive strengths, Jay's teacher "still responded to Jay as though he were less than capable" (p. xiii). The teacher's beliefs about Jay's abilities and, consequently, his academic needs were premised on a deficit model and reinforced by labels applied to him by the schooling process, leading her to discount evidence of his achievements as somehow immaterial. Although perhaps unintentional, the actions of his teacher served to limit the possibilities for Jay's success.

A practice exists in the United States of using school as a location in which to label students according to some perceived "ability" and separate them into various levels of coursework rather than see the potential for success that lies in every student (Oakes 2005). As this article's opening quote describes, this approach has led to practices in the mathematics classroom that often keep students from the mathematics rather than get them into it (Ellis 2007). Efforts to reform our teaching of mathematics such that a broader range of students have access to high standards and are supported in reaching those standards are often at odds with this practice or habit of mind. When thinking about the idea of differentiation in the mathematics classroom, how it is undertaken must be carefully considered—what are the assumptions and beliefs from which teachers work to differentiate instruction? This article is intended to stimulate readers to examine the positions from which their own efforts at differentiation are enacted. Specifically, notions of ability are examined as social constructions

When thinking about the idea of differentiation in the mathematics classroom, how it is undertaken must be carefully considered—what are the assumptions and beliefs from which teachers work to differentiate instruction?

that have a big impact on how efforts to differentiate instruction come to be crafted.

Since the early 1900s, school mathematics in the United States has offered a convenient location for the separation of students by so-called "ability" (Ellis 2008). Although concern about the overall mathematical knowledge of all students has become greater and greater in recent years (Diaz and Lord 2005; National Commission on Mathematics and Science Teaching for the Twenty-first Century 2000; National Council of Teachers of Mathematics [NCTM] 2000; U.S. Department of Education 2003), much of the energy being directed toward mathematics education remains focused on determining students' placement within a variety of leveled courses, planning and implementing separate curricula, and measuring the resulting variations in learning outcomes (Booher-Jennings 2005; Diamond and Spillane 2004). Although these efforts may be socially sought after, they are in large part educationally counterproductive (Ayalon and Gamoran 2000; Boaler, Wiliam, and Brown 2000; Oakes 2005). As long as outcomes in mathematics achievement as measured by standardized examinations (and the resulting inferences about students' abilities in mathematics) continue to be correlated with such demographic markers as economic status, race, and ZIP code, the educational mission of schooling—that of supporting all students in reaching their full potential—has yet to be fulfilled.

At issue are conceptions of mathematical ability and students' potential and the impact that these factors have on teachers' decisions about how best to serve their students. Ample research has documented the ways in which poor academic performance among low-income and African American and Latino students is problematized such that students' characteristics and backgrounds are blamed, whereas such factors as opportunities to learn and access to information are ignored (Diversity in Mathematics Education Center for Learning and Teaching 2007; Oakes et al. 1997; Rubin 2008). Such deficit perspectives persist despite teachers' commonly stated belief that all students can succeed in school (Wilson and Corbett 2007).

Activating Students' Potential

Hearing talk about students who are of "low ability," or who "don't care" about learning, or who "can't do math" leads me to think back to my experiences as a teacher of mathematics in low- to middle-income communities with students who were diverse not only ethnically, economically, and linguistically but also with respect to their existing knowledge of mathematics and their preferred learning modalities (e.g., visual, tactile). In my classroom students who did not care to do mathematics, who were not proficient in English, whose abilities in mathematics had been deemed to be low, somehow found themselves learning mathematics. The cause of this apparent aberration was grounded in my refusal to base expectations for students' achievement on the labels applied to them by schools and society.

As a case in point, Alonso[1] was in my seventh-grade mathematics class along with twenty-four other students whose existing knowledge of mathematics was tenuous at best. The class average on their sixth-grade state mathematics examination placed them at the thirtieth percentile, far from what I considered their potential. Alonso's prior achievement in mathematics was well below that of his peers, in the single digits, a result that seemed inexorably linked with his being labeled as having low ability. Although I realized that he lacked *proficiency* with many mathematical concepts and skills, I did not equate this lack with Alonso's having a low *ability* to do mathematics. In fact, as I got to know Alonso, I learned that he had become accustomed to being left alone in class as long as he was not causing a distraction—left alone and not encouraged to learn to do mathematics (see Rousseau and Tate [2003] for research documenting how students from certain groups are "allowed to fail"). For me this neglect was at the root of his low achievement in mathematics.

Over the course of the two years that Alonso and his peers were in my mathematics class, through the seventh and eighth grades, they grew in every way imaginable—physically, socially, and, of course, academically. The class mean on the state mathematics examination increased to the sixty-third percentile, and Alonso's, to the sixty-fifth. Even more important, the students became doers of mathematics who communicated their thinking, challenged one another to justify strategies and outcomes, and strove to make sense of mathematics. This improvement took place in spite of the labels that had been applied to them by the schooling system and by society. These students' progress was made possible by my connecting mathematics with their lives through contextualized problems; providing multiple pathways to learning important concepts, including the use of visual models; requiring them to achieve proficiency in prerequisite skills while at the same time engaging them in learning grade-level concepts; and holding them accountable for making progress that reflected their potential to make sense of mathematics. Their success was due to the phenomenal response by my students and their supportive families to the challenge to bring their proficiency in mathematics up to and above benchmarks set by the state standards.

Essential to this success was a perspective that a fundamental aspect of a teacher's job is to hold high expectations of every student's potential and to create possibilities for all students to learn in ways that respect who they are and recognize their strengths as learners. Bransford, Brown, and Cocking (2000, p. 6), in their landmark publication *How People Learn: Brain, Mind, Experience, and School*, state quite powerfully,

> Learning research suggests that there are new ways to introduce students to traditional subjects, such as mathematics, science, history and literature, and that these new approaches make it possible for the majority of individuals to develop a deep understanding of important subject matter.

---

1. This is a pseudonym.

Although I realized that he lacked *proficiency* with many mathematical concepts and skills, I did not equate this lack with Alonso's having a low *ability* to do mathematics.

Essential to this success was a perspective that a fundamental aspect of a teacher's job is to hold high expectations of every student's potential and to create possibilities for all students to learn in ways that respect who they are and recognize their strengths as learners.

This philosophy lies at the heart of efforts to make mathematics accessible to all students, a concept exemplified by the cases and strategies shared by the authors in this book. Rather than continue the legacy of separation and leveled expectations, teachers of mathematics must learn to recognize and teach to students' strengths.

Problematizing Differentiation

The *Oxford English Dictionary* (Simpson and Wiener 1989) defines *differentiate* as "To make or render different; to constitute the difference in or between; to distinguish." The term *differentiate* derives from *different*, meaning "not of the same kind; not alike; of other nature, form, or quality" (Simpson and Wiener 1989). The underlying concept within these terms is that of making comparisons with a standard or norm and recognizing objects that fall outside that norm. That "differentiate" came into common use in the mid- to late-1800s (Simpson and Wiener 1989) is indicative of Western imperialistic and rationalistic thought of an era in which dominant groups sought to bring under control those who were "other" than the norm (Willinsky 1998). Given this historical perspective, care must be taken when using a term such as *differentiation of instruction* if the aim is to give all students greater opportunity for meaningful learning to take place.

Indeed, when examining its use in education, one finds that differentiation of instruction is characterized in multiple and often discrepant ways. One well-known scholar of differentiation, Carol Tomlinson (2000), contends, "Whenever a teacher reaches out to an individual or small group to vary his or her teaching in order to create the best learning experience possible, that teacher is differentiating instruction." The central idea within Tomlinson's depiction of differentiation is to *vary one's actions as a teacher to meet the needs of students*. Note that the focus here is on changing instructional practices, moving beyond the standard, or normative, habits that characterize mathematics teaching (e.g., teacher-led lecture and demonstration followed by students' individual work on rote procedures; see Stigler and Hiebert [1997]; Weiss et al. [2003]).

In contrast with a focus on changing teachers' actions, Ayalon (2006) describes how differentiation is often viewed from a curricular perspective: "[A] differentiated curriculum enables students to enroll in courses that are congruent with their interests and abilities. The rationale behind level differentiation and formal tracking underscores the diversity in students' abilities and the need to offer programs that correspond to that diversity" (p. 1188). From this perspective, differentiation involves *changing the curriculum in response to students' perceived abilities*. Particularly in school mathematics, with its history of providing inequitable access to content on the basis of perceived ability, this latter take on differentiation is all too easily embraced—but should be vociferously avoided! Although teacher educators often frame differentiation much as Tomlinson does—as requiring teachers to respond to students' needs to make content accessible—in practice the curriculum is often changed because of perceived differences

The central idea within Tomlinson's depiction of differentiation is to vary one's actions as a teacher to meet the needs of students.

in students' abilities. I argue that the latter of these responses to differentiation is a consequence of the term itself that, together with a belief that mathematical ability is both accurately measurable and unevenly distributed, promotes actions that work against our efforts to create classroom environments in which all students learn meaningful mathematics.

Creating Possibilities for Students' Success

The challenge, then, is to move one's focus from "ability" to "possibility" by getting to know students' strengths and preferences with respect to learning modalities, then implementing lessons that activate those strengths and build from existing knowledge. Meeting this challenge requires a new stance toward teaching mathematics that is premised on creating possibilities for students' learning, a perspective that expects students to be successful when provided access to important ideas and that furnishes support in making sense of these ideas. This sort of differentiation, reflective of Tomlinson's definition, shifts teachers' attention away from activities that construct students as able or unable, directing attention instead toward strategies and situations that allow access for all students to learn mathematics. Too many "Jays" and "Alonsos" in our classrooms fall victim to traditional habits of teaching mathematics. Instead, our efforts to make content meaningful and accessible must activate the tremendous potential that lies within all students.

REFERENCES

Alayon, Hanna. "Nonhierarchical Curriculum Differentiation and Inequality in Achievement: A Different Story or More of the Same?" *Teachers College Record* 108, no. 8 (June 2006): 1186–1213.

Ayalon, Hanna, and Adam Gamoran. "Stratification in Academic Secondary Programs and Educational Inequality in Israel and the United States." *Comparative Education Review* 44, no. 1 (February 2000): 54–80.

Boaler, Joan, Dylan Wiliam, and Margaret Brown. "Students' Experiences of Ability Grouping: Disaffection, Polarization and the Construction of Failure." *British Educational Research Journal* 26, no. 5 (December 2000): 631–48.

Booher-Jennings, Jennifer. "Below the Bubble: 'Educational Triage' and the Texas Accountability System." *American Educational Research Journal* 42, no. 2 (Summer 2005):231–68.

Bransford, John D., Ann L. Brown, and Rodney R. Cocking. *How People Learn: Brain, Mind, Experience, and School.* Washington, D.C.: National Academies Press, 2000.

Collins, Kathleen M. *Ability Profiling and School Failure: One Child's Struggle to Be Seen as Competent.* Mahwah, N.J.: Lawrence Erlbaum Associates, 2003.

Diamond, John B., and James P. Spillane. "High-Stakes Accountability in Urban Elementary Schools: Challenging or Reproducing Inequality?" *Teachers College Record* 106, no. 6 (June 2004): 1145–76.

Diaz, Alicia, and Joan Lord. *Focusing on Student Performance through Accountability.* Atlanta, Ga.: Southern Regional Education Board, 2005.

Diversity in Mathematics Education Center for Learning and Teaching. "Culture, Race, Power, and Mathematics Education." In *Second Handbook of Research on Mathematics Teaching and Learning,* edited by Frank J. Lester Jr., pp. 405–33. Charlotte, N.C.: Information Age Publishing, 2007.

Ellis, Mark W. "President's Choice: Constructing a Personal Understanding of Mathematics: Making the Pieces Fit." *Mathematics Teacher* 100, no. 8 (April 2007): 516–22.

———. "Leaving No Child Behind Yet Allowing None Too Far Ahead: Ensuring (In)Equity in Mathematics Education through the Science of Measurement and Instruction." *Teachers College Record* 110, no. 6 (2008): 1330–56.

Gorgorió, Núria, and Núria Planas. "Cultural Distance and Identities-in-Construction within the Multicultural Mathematics Classroom." *Zentralblatt für Didaktik der Mathematik* 37, no. 2 (2005): 64–71.

National Commission on Mathematics and Science Teaching for the Twenty-first Century. *Before It's Too Late*. Washington, D.C.: U. S. Department of Education, 2000.

National Council of Teachers of Mathematics (NCTM). *Principles and Standards for School Mathematics*. Reston, Va.: NCTM, 2000.

Oakes, Jeannie. *Keeping Track: How Schools Structure Inequality*. 2nd ed. New Haven, Conn.: Yale University Press, 2005.

Oakes, Jeannie, Amy Stuart Wells, Makeba Jones, and Amanda Datnow. "Detracking: The Social Construction of Ability, Cultural Politics, and Resistance to Reform." *Teachers' College Record* 98, no. 3 (1997): 482–510.

Rousseau, Celia, and William F. Tate. "No Time Like the Present: Reflecting on Equity in School Mathematics." *Theory into Practice* 42, no. 3 (Summer 2003): 210–16.

Rubin, Beth H. "Detracking in Context: How Local Constructions of Ability Complicate Equity-Geared Reform." *Teachers College Record* 110, no. 3 (2008): 646–99. www.tcrecord.org/Content.asp?ContentId=14603.

Simpson, John A., and Edmund S. C. Wiener, eds. *Oxford English Dictionary*. 2nd ed. New York: Oxford University Press, 1989.

Stigler, James W., and James Hiebert. "Understanding and Improving Classroom Mathematics Instruction: An Overview of the TIMSS Video Study." *Phi Delta Kappan* 79, no. 1 (1997): 14–21.

Tomlinson, Carol. "Differentiation of Instruction in the Elementary Grades." ERIC Digest (August 2000). Document No. ED0-PS-00-7. Available at ericece.org.

United States Department of Education. "Proven Methods: The Facts about … Math Achievement." www.ed.gov/nclb/methods/math/math.pdf.

Weiss, Iris R., Joan D. Pasley, P. Sean Smith, Eric R. Banilower, and Daniel C. Heck. *Looking inside the Classroom: A Study of K–12 Mathematics and Science Education in the United States*. Chapel Hill, N.C.: Horizon Research, 2003. www.horizon-research.com/insidetheclassroom/reports/looking/.

Willinsky, John. *Learning to Divide the World: Education at Empire's End*. Minneapolis, Minn.: University of Minnesota Press, 1998.

Wilson, Bruce, and Dick Corbett. "Students' Perspectives on Good Teaching: Implications for Adult Reform Behavior." In *International Handbook of Student Experience in Elementary and Secondary School*, edited by Dennis Theissen and Alison Cook-Sather, pp. 283–311. Dordrecht, Netherlands: Springer, 2007.

10

Why Discourse Deserves Our Attention!

Beth Herbel-Eisenmann
Michelle Cirillo
Kathryn Skowronski

WE HAVE often assumed that our secondary school mathematics teacher preparation did not address language use because it was something that was taken for granted. Our first exposure to the idea of classroom discourse came from reading the discourse standards (NCTM 1991, p. 34):

> The discourse of a classroom—the ways of representing, thinking, talking, agreeing, disagreeing—is central to what students learn about mathematics as a domain of human inquiry with characteristic ways of knowing. Discourse is both the way ideas are exchanged and what the ideas entail: Who talks? About what? In what ways? What do people write, what do they record, and why? What questions are important? How do ideas change? Whose ideas and ways of thinking are valued? Who determines when to end a discussion?... Discourse entails fundamental issues about knowledge: What makes something true or reasonable in mathematics? How can we figure out whether or not something makes sense?

This quotation alone made us think about myriad issues that we had not considered previously: How does mathematics as a domain of "human inquiry" play out in a secondary school mathematics classroom? In what ways do we *value* ideas and ways of thinking when we teach mathematics? How does our classroom discourse entail "fundamental issues about knowledge?"

In our quest to understand more about classroom discourse, we have been involved in reading and discussion groups[1] focused on mathematics classroom discourse. We have come to understand one thing more than anything else: discourse is something to which all mathematics teachers and teacher educators need to pay more explicit and conscious attention. In this

---

1. This article is based on work supported by the National Science Foundation (NSF Grant No. 0347906, Beth Herbel-Eisenmann, principal investigator). Any opinions, findings, and conclusions or recommendations expressed in this material are those of the authors and do not necessarily reflect the views of the NSF.

We give at least four reasons why we believe classroom discourse is something that needs more careful and thoughtful attention, especially in mathematics, where achievement gaps are an issue and where arguments have been made that mathematics is a "gatekeeper" for higher education.

article, we give at least four reasons why we believe classroom discourse is something that needs more careful and thoughtful attention, especially in mathematics, where achievement gaps are an issue and where arguments have been made that mathematics is a "gatekeeper" for higher education. These four reasons are as follows: (1) mathematics is a specialized form of literacy, (2) spoken language is a primary mode of teaching and learning, (3) the particular context in which language is used plays a role in what is appropriate to say and do, and (4) language is intimately related to culture and identity. We discuss each of these reasons in the next four sections and then make some suggestions for how to use this information for professional development.

Mathematics Is a Specialized Form of Literacy

Literacy typically includes speaking, writing, reading, listening, and viewing. These skills are often different in everyday life from the literacy skills that we teach in schools, and some children come to school with home-literacy skills that are more like those expected at school. In fact, as students progress through their schooling experience (Schleppegrell 2004, p. 22),

> the tasks they are asked to do become more and more dependent on the control of a wide range of linguistic resources. While these ways of making meaning may appear to set up barriers for children from backgrounds that have not prepared them for participation in this context, the ways of meaning are integral to accomplishing the goals of schooling. Learning and language are closely related, and for success at school, students need to come to understand the context of schooling and the linguistic choices that realize that context.

These literacy skills and their increasing demands for students as they progress in school also apply to mathematics. Our students must develop these skills to be recognized as mathematically literate people. Speaking, writing, reading, listening, and viewing *mathematics*, however, require a specialized form of literacy, and accordingly, these processes need to be distinguished from nonmathematical uses. Furthermore, because reading, speaking, and writing in mathematics can be more stilted and structured than in other academic areas, the difference between students' home literacy and school mathematics literacy can potentially be greater than the difference between students' home literacy and their literacy in other content areas.

Because reading, speaking, and writing in mathematics can be more stilted and structured than in other academic areas, the difference between students' home literacy and school mathematics literacy can potentially be greater than the difference between students' home literacy and their literacy in other content areas.

Language can be divided up into different-sized units (e.g., words, phrases, sentences, and discourses [Fillmore and Snow 2000]). Each unit needs to be attended to in the teaching and learning of mathematics because the mathematical context makes them *different* from when they are used outside a mathematical context. Words imported into mathematics, for example, can have quite different meanings than they do in their everyday use (Thompson and Rubenstein 2000). And the way we write and talk about words in mathematics can make them even more difficult to learn.

For instance, students have probably used the word *sign* many times outside their mathematics classroom in reference to such things as a "stop sign" or "signing" their names on a sheet of paper. In mathematics, however, we talk about the "sign" of a number, meaning that it is in a positive or negative direction from zero on a number line. We could also use the word *sine*, which sounds the same but means something quite different. To add further complication, when we write "sine" or when we use calculators, we write or look for *sin*, which, again, has a completely different meaning outside the mathematics classroom. Explicit discussions about these kinds of nuances in mathematical language may be needed to make certain that all students understand the tacit differences. (For information about how students might learn vocabulary in meaningful ways, see Herbel-Eisenmann [2002].)

Many of the mathematical processes that we want students to learn (e.g., communicating, reasoning, proving, representing) are processes that students also use in other content areas and are especially important to emphasize in diverse classrooms. These mathematical processes require us to put words, sentences, and discourses together in very specific ways that make them mathematical rather than something else. For example, although students may learn how to formulate a debate in their English classrooms, the argumentation that is particular to mathematics is not the same. We use certain words and structure verbal mathematical arguments in ways that are quite distinct from how we put arguments together in everyday life and in other subject areas. Our interactions with students help them understand what constitutes an acceptable mathematical explanation. That is, we need to make clear to students that a mathematical explanation must be an explanation that does more than just agree with someone because she or he has high status in the classroom (Yackel and Cobb 1996). It also must be more than just a procedural description if we want students to develop a high-level mathematical argument (Kazemi and Stipek 2001).

Researchers who study mathematical argumentation in classrooms in which mathematical inquiry is central have drawn on Toulmin's (1958) discussion of claims, grounds, warrants, and backings. They contend that when students are involved in making claims and defending them against other positions, higher-level thinking is developed (O'Connor and Michaels 1993, 1996). They also show that mathematical arguments require different forms of language that are subtle and complex. For instance, students who make high-quality mathematical arguments use appropriate warrants and backings for claims, support and illustrate claims through using visual representations, expand and make explicit ideas that others have left implicit, and address the mathematical flaws in others people's arguments (Forman et al. 1998).

The *metarules* of mathematical arguments, proofs, and explanations are often learned without deliberate planning by teachers and without being consciously considered by anyone (Sfard 2000). A teacher can point out that in a two-column proof, however, the only kinds of statements that should appear in the column of reasons are definitions, postulates, and theorems. The tacit nature of these mathematical forms sometimes makes them difficult for *all* students to take up. In some instances, the teacher must make these implicit qualities of mathematical language use more explicit. The teacher can make these hidden rules transparent by "stepping out" (Rittenhouse 1998) of the mathematical conversation to comment on what is being done and why. This kind of explicit attention to linguistic form is something that Delpit (1988) argued is needed in discourse-based teaching.

Lubienski (2000) provided a vivid image of how the poor and working-class students she taught struggled in a discussion-intensive mathematics classroom. Her findings showed some ways in which *middle-class* students' ways of learning might be more aligned with the classroom envisioned by the NCTM *Standards* documents (NCTM 1989, 1991, 2000). This unintended consequence of reform-oriented teaching requires that educators "find ways to teach students the discursive skills necessary to thrive in discussion-intensive classrooms" (Lubienski 2000, p. 399).

Additionally, using mathematical explanation and argumentation may cause students to be uncomfortable if they believe that only one correct solution exists to any mathematics problem. In fact, in students' everyday lives, argumentation—or arguing in general—is typically considered rude and unsociable. This belief can create challenges to using this valuable process in the mathematics classroom (Lampert, Rittenhouse, and Crumbaugh 1996). (For more information about creating a context for mathematical argumentation, see Wood [1999]; Stein [2001].)

Spoken Language Is Primary to Teaching and Learning

Spoken language is the primary medium that we use in classroom instruction. It is also one of the ways that students are asked to demonstrate what they know in the classroom. As teachers and teacher educators, we need to be able to help our students restructure learning contexts by fostering the "build-up of increasingly rich stores of such 'common knowledge'" (Cazden 2001, p. 75). Our role as more mathematically knowledgeable people than students allows us to model mathematical practices, such as mathematical argumentation, for our students. Our role as teachers in charge of the classroom allows us to structure the learning environment in ways that provide opportunities for students to learn. For example, the kinds of questions we ask, how we pace lessons, how long we wait for students to answer a question, how long we wait *after* a student responds to a question, and how we structure activities are all ways that illustrate to students the type of discourse that is acceptable in our classrooms. In addition, really *hearing* what students *mean* is the key to analyzing what students might know and understand. *Hearing* students also allows us to decide which teaching moves might be most helpful in pushing our students' understandings forward. For example, Moschkovich (1999) has shown how teachers of English language learners can use revoicing to help support the development of mathematical language. Teachers can strategically

> Our role as more mathematically knowledgeable people than students allows us to model mathematical practices, such as mathematical argumentation, for our students.

ask students to revoice either their own or other students' claims about mathematics so as to practice mathematical language, clarify meaning, and engage students in the discussion. (For further readings about revoicing, see O'Connor and Michaels [1993, 1996]; Forman et al. [1998]; Chapin, O'Connor, and Anderson [2003].)

Cazden (2001, p. 60) pointed out the tension between students' thinking (knowledge) and interaction with others (spoken language):

> It is never easy to talk about relationships between individual (silent) thinking processes and the dyadic or group (often noisy) interactions in the classroom. But because that relationship is at the heart of student learning and must therefore be at the heart of teachers' planning, we have to try.

We often evaluate students on the basis of what they say or what they write. Our judgments can have massive consequences for our students, from their self-confidence in their ability to learn to the decision whether they get promoted to the next grade. Many differences exist across cultures in the kinds of linguistic behaviors thought to be appropriate at different ages (Fillmore and Snow 2000). Students from underrepresented groups often get placed in lower-track mathematics classrooms because they speak differently. For example, although vocabulary is often viewed as the main challenge to bilingual mathematics learners, an emphasis on vocabulary gives a narrow view of mathematical communication (Moschkovich 2007). We need to understand "different sources of variation in language use" (Fillmore and Snow 2000, p. 9) to make better assessments of students' learning. If we do not recognize that other ways of speaking and writing are valid for making meaning, then we risk undermining the "students' confidence in their own communicative abilities" (Fillmore and Snow 2000, p. 5). In a later section, we address further the importance of language, culture, and identity.

Context at Many Levels Shapes Our Language

Classrooms are very specific contexts in which we interact in particular ways. For example, if we are walking with a friend and ask her what time it is, we would never respond to her answer with "That's right, it *is* 1:00!" Yet we make such statements in classrooms all the time because, in the context of a classroom, this kind of statement, which *I*nitiates a question to which we already know the answer, gets a *R*esponse, and then *E*valuates what the person said (*I-R-E;* Mehan [1979]), is considered an acceptable comment to make. Researchers (Stigler and Hiebert 1999) have shown that *I-R-E* is one of the most prevalent interaction patterns in classrooms. In other settings or in other cultures, such an interaction might be considered rude, inappropriate, or demeaning.

Additionally, throughout the course of a lesson, many different activities take place, and each of these is a context that requires different language patterns. For example, the language patterns that occur when a

If we do not recognize that other ways of speaking and writing are valid for making meaning, then we risk undermining the "students' confidence in their own communicative abilities" (Fillmore and Snow 2000, p. 5).

Throughout a lesson, many different activities take place, and each is a context that requires different language patterns. For example, the language patterns that occur when a teacher is guiding students through rote exercises are likely different from those when they are working on a challenging problem.

teacher is guiding students through rote exercises are likely different from those when they are working on a challenging problem. Being aware of the impact of these different contexts and the ways in which they may or may not provide opportunities for students to "display" intelligence and language is very important: Whereas in the previous section we focused more on how the mathematical context makes a difference in language use, in this section we focus on how other kinds of classroom contexts influence language use.

Classroom behavior is directed by rules and routines that are implicitly taught, tacitly agreed on, and mutually negotiated. Some of the tacit rules of classroom discourse that have been described by linguists include the following (Edwards and Mercer 1987):

- Teachers can ask questions.

- Teachers often know the answers to the questions they ask.

- When questions are repeated, it means that the answer that was given was incorrect.

As Cazden (2001, p. 82) pointed out,

> In traditional classrooms, the most important asymmetry in the rights and obligations of teachers and students is control over the right to speak. To describe the difference in the bluntest of terms, teachers have the role-given right to speak any time and to any person; they can fill any silence or interrupt any speaker; they can speak to a student anywhere in the room and in any volume or tone of voice. No one has the right to object. But not all teachers assume such rights and few live by such rules all the time.

As we suggested in the previous section on mathematics as a form of literacy, if students are to be successful in classrooms, these tacit rules also need to be made explicit to all students. As Cazden and Mehan (1992) explained, students must recognize varying contexts and shift their language use multiple times throughout the day, and even within a particular lesson. For example, when we have students working in small groups, we want them to talk to one another; when they are answering questions on homework, however, we typically do not want them to do so. We may not explicitly tell students what kind of talk is appropriate in each of these settings. Recognizing these shifts and talking explicitly about the different norms in each of these contexts can help all students be more successful in the activities we are asking them to do. If students do not recognize these contexts as different, they may be less likely to display the kinds of norms for interaction we would like to see. We often do not draw attention to the classroom rules and routines in ways that would make them apparent to students.

Unless we become more aware of our tacit rules and routines, we will be unable make them more explicit or to change them. As we mentioned previously, whether we are aware of it or not, the *I-R-E* pattern is a default pattern in most classrooms. Alternative patterns require quite different norms from some of the other patterns described in this section. For example, real discussion "requires a slower pace, relaxation of the teacher's turn-taking control, and departure from the three-part *I-R-E* sequence" (Cazden and Mehan 1992, p. 51). It also requires that we analyze students' responses and make students' thinking and contributions central. Another alternative pattern that we might use includes "focusing" (Wood 1998; Herbel-Eisenmann and Breyfogle 2005) students' thinking. In this pattern, we ask questions that allow us to understand students' thinking and to highlight salient points in their solution that might be helpful to other students. Additional alternatives may need to take students' cultural backgrounds into consideration.

Language Is Intimately Tied to People's Culture and Identity

> *Our language embraces us long before we are defined by any other medium of identity. In our mother's womb we hear and feel the sounds, the rhythms, the cadences of our "mother tongue." We learn to associate contentment with certain qualities of voice and physical disequilibrium with others. Our home language is as viscerally tied to our beings as existence itself.... It is no wonder that out first language becomes intimately connected to our identity.*

—Lisa Delpit and Joanne Kilgour Dowdy, *The Skin That We Speak*

The fourth and, we believe, most important reason that mathematics teachers need to pay more explicit attention to classroom discourse is that language and people's culture and identity are intimately tied to each other. Schools are the first large institutions from which children leave their families in their home neighborhoods and are expected to participate individually and publicly. School is a multicultural encounter with both teachers and students belonging to diverse groups differentiated by such variables as age, social class, gender, race, and ethnicity (Banks and Banks 1995). As a result, students do not come to school with exactly the same "home discourses," and home discourse does not necessarily map onto "school discourse." In fact, some home discourses are much closer to school discourses than others. (See Heath [1983] for information about how students' communities teach children different "ways with words.")

In conventional classroom discourse, students are expected to listen quietly while the teacher talks, responding only with the established rules, such as one person speaking at a time. In addition, students are expected to speak in complete sentences, use proper vocabulary and grammar, be brief and to the point, and address only the specific topic defined by the teacher. The traditional structure of mathematics classes constrains opportunities for diverse cultural traditions to serve as classroom resources. For example, Brenner (1998, p. 215) stated that—

> there is substantial evidence that the participant structure of a traditional classroom, that is, the roles and responsibilities

Students do not come to school with exactly the same "home discourses," and home discourse does not necessarily map onto "school discourse."

assigned to the different persons, can act as an inhibiting factor to children who come from a culture that stresses different participant structures than those found at school.

The process of learning mathematics can be disrupted when a mismatch occurs between the cultures of home and school.

Although many students from the middle and upper classes come to school with tools to participate in the mainstream cultural discourse, students from poor or minority families may operate within cultures that do not carry the same power codes or rules (Malloy and Malloy 1998). In fact, school practices may actively disregard the personal and cultural knowledge of students, focusing instead on school knowledge. The sorting practices that occur in schools (e.g., standardized testing and tracking) are designed to exclude rather than include. Instead, teachers should attempt to gain an in-depth understanding of their students' backgrounds and the relationship between their cultures and their learning (Malloy and Malloy 1998). For example, getting to know students' backgrounds can allow us to modify our curriculum materials to make mathematics problems interesting and applicable to students' lives, and it can help us assist students in using mathematics in critical ways (Gutstein 2006).

In today's multicultural classrooms, the role of different ways of knowing and doing mathematics emerges from cultural differences among students (Schleppegrell 2007). Recognizing these different ways of knowing and of using language, however, can be a challenge when dealing with the subject of mathematics, whose language is rife with metarules and specialized vocabulary that are not necessarily compatible with everyday language. As a result, the teacher, the instrumental leader of the classroom discourse, may make decisions regarding what contributions are heard that, although justifiable from a mathematical point of view, may silence and marginalize diverse out-of-school types of discourse (Lampert and Cobb 2003).

To work with the many cultural differences in the classroom, Gay (2000, p. 109) advocated for *culturally responsive teaching:*

> … teachers should not merely make girls talk more like boys, or boys talk more like girls, or all individuals within and across ethnic groups talk like each other…. Instead [teachers] must be mindful that communication styles are multidimensional and multimodal, shaped by many different influences. Although culture is paramount among these, other critical influences include ethnic affiliation, gender, social class, personality, individuality, and experiential context.

Gay (2000) illustrated this point by explaining how, in the African American culture, participatory entry into conversations is gained through personal assertiveness, the strength of the impulse to be involved, and the persuasive power of the point the individual wishes to make, not through waiting for an "authority" to grant permission. Because many teachers view this type of participation as "rude," "inconsiderate," "disruptive," and "speaking out of turn," they might penalize students for this type of behavior, thus discouraging them from participation in the conversation (Gay 2000). Au and Jordan (working with native Hawaiian children [1981]) and Warren and Rosebery (working with Creole children of Haitian descent [1995]) also illustrate how the development of academic knowledge can be fostered through teaching that clearly recognizes and builds from students' cultural resources. Because communication, the medium of teaching and learning, is linked with culture, teachers must attend to it in more conscious and explicit ways.

Suggestions for Professional Development

Mathematics teachers and teacher educators have many ways to come to understand students' language use and continually learn how to improve classroom discourse practices. Owing to space limitations, we discuss two ways in which we have been involved in such work: reading and discussing professional literature on classroom discourse with small groups of mathematics teachers, teacher leaders, and university faculty; and designing and conducting action research projects related to classroom discourse. The process of reading literature can help raise consciousness about the roles of words, language, and discourse in teaching and learning, as well as help mathematics teachers and teacher educators understand students' home discourse (Herbel-Eisenmann et al. 2007). In fact, the primary reason we wrote this article is that the teachers with whom we collaborate believe that mathematics teachers need to know the information they learned through reading literature related to classroom discourse.

Raising consciousness, however, does not always lead to the changes needed to support diverse learners in mathematics classrooms (Sleeter 1997). Fundamental changes that involve an alignment of new beliefs with tacit discourse practices need to take place. Teachers are asked repeatedly to change how they teach, but they rarely have worthwhile data that invites them to do so. Without a close examination of discourse practices in mathematics classrooms, teachers may not fully realize the goal of teaching to high standards for all students.

Science and mathematics teachers have found action research to be a powerful way to make positive changes related to language use in classrooms (Gallas 1995; Gallas et al. 1996; Lee 2006; Grant and McGraw 2006; Wells 2001; Huhn, Huhn, and Lamb 2006). Action research has also helped teachers build understandings about students' home discourses so as to improve their classroom practices (Ballenger 1997, 1999; Ballenger and Rosebery 2003). Action research encourages reflection on, and changes to, teaching practices. By collecting evidence of their own discourse practices, teachers can investigate their enacted beliefs in the context of their own classroom. Action research provides the opportunity needed for teachers to investigate the social influences found in their classrooms, because teachers can audiotape or videotape class sessions and review them to reflect on their discourse practices. Some teacher-researchers (e.g., Ballenger [1997]) strongly suggest transcribing sections of classroom talk because they believe this process allowed them to understand their

Action research provides the opportunity needed for teachers to investigate the social influences found in their classrooms, because teachers can audiotape or videotape class sessions and review them to reflect on their discourse practices.

classroom discourse in ways that taking part in it and watching it did not. Reeves (1990, p. 446) stated that "without the action research, the social dimensions of the role of language in mathematics learning would be difficult to appreciate." For example, the teacher-researchers with whom we collaborate have extensively discussed how their language controls both social and mathematical processes in their classrooms. They decided that, to engage more students, they need to attend consciously to what, when, and how they control students' turn-taking, mathematical sharing, and other aspects of their classroom discourse. They also realized that many of the implicit rules that shape their classroom discourse need to be made more explicit to students so that all students understand how to participate in ways that support their learning. Prior to reading the literature on classroom discourse, however, they had not considered these issues as needing attention in the same ways as they now do.

Conclusion

Fillmore and Snow (2000, p. 22) pointed out that because academic language is learned through exposure and practice over time, teachers—

> must recognize that a focus on language—no matter what subject they are teaching—is crucial. They must engage children in classroom discussions of subject matter that are more and more sophisticated in form and content. And they must know enough about language to discuss it and to support its development in their students.

Here we have come full circle. As the quotation above indicates, we need to know enough about language to be able to discuss it and support its development in our classrooms. Little of this information was given to us in our teacher preparation, however, and the attempts that were made to help us understand it through professional development were not focused on mathematical contexts in ways that were meaningful to us. After reading extensively on the topic, we strongly believe that discourse needs to be a primary focus in mathematics classrooms—especially if we want to work toward more equitable representation of all students in higher levels of mathematics.

If we are going to support all students' success in mathematics education, all four parts of this argument warrant our attention:

- mathematical literacies and how they are distinct from other forms of literacy;

- relationships between spoken language and the roles we play as the teacher;

- how different classroom contexts carry different norms and rules for interaction; and

- relationships between students' home discourse practices and school discourse practices.

By engaging with this more complex view of language use, we believe that, as mathematics teachers and teacher educators, we can more consciously pay attention to language choices and hear students' meanings. In turn, hearing students and responding with high expectations and explicit support can help *all* students learn mathematics more successfully.

REFERENCES

Au, Kathryn H., and Cathie Jordan. "Teaching Reading to Hawaiian Children: Finding a Culturally Appropriate Solution." In *Culture in the Bilingual Classroom: Studies in Classroom Ethnography,* edited by Henry T. Trueba, Grace P. Guthrie, and Kathryn H. Au, pp. 139–52. Rowley, Mass.: Newbury House, 1981.

Banks, Cherry A. McGee, and James A. Banks. "Equity Pedagogy: An Essential Component of Multicultural Education." *Theory into Practice* 34, no. 3 (1995): 152–58.

Ballenger, Cynthia. "Social Identities, Moral Narratives, Scientific Argumentation: Science Talk in a Bilingual Classroom." *Language and Education* 11, no. 1 (1997): 1–14.

———. *Teaching Other People's Children: Literacy and Learning in a Bilingual Classroom.* New York: Teachers College Press, 1999.

Ballenger, Cynthia, and Ann Rosebery. "What Counts as Teacher Research? Investigating the Scientific and Mathematical Ideas of Children from Culturally Diverse Backgrounds." *Teachers College Record* 105, no. 2 (2003): 297–314.

Brenner, Mary E. "Addition Cognition to the Formula for Culturally Relevant Instruction in Mathematics." *Anthropology and Education Quarterly* 29, no. 2 (1998): 214–44.

Cazden, Courtney B. *Classroom Discourse: The Language of Teaching and Learning.* 2nd ed. Portsmouth, N.H.: Heinemann Educational Books, 2001.

Cazden, Courtney B., and Hugh Mehan. "Principles from Sociology and Anthropology: Context, Code, Classroom, and Culture." In *Knowledge Base for the Beginning Teacher,* edited by Maynard C. Reynolds, pp.47–57. Toronto, Ontario: Pergamon Press, 1992.

Chapin, Susan H., Mary C. O'Connor, and Nancy C. Anderson. *Classroom Discussions: Using Math Talk to Help Students Learn.* Sausalito, Calif.: Math Solutions Publications, 2003.

Delpit, Lisa. "The Silenced Dialogue: Power and Pedagogy in Educating Other People's Children." *Harvard Educational Review* 58 (1988): 280–97.

Delpit, Lisa, and Joanne Kilgour Dowdy, eds. *The Skin That We Speak: Thoughts on Language and Culture in the Classroom.* New York: New Press, 2002.

Edwards, Derek, and Neil Mercer. *Common Knowledge.* New York: Methuen, 1987.

Fillmore, Lily W., and Catherine E. Snow. *What Teachers Need to Know about Language.* Washington, D.C.: Office of Educational Research and Improvement, Center for Applied Linguistics, 2000.

Forman, Ellice A., Jorge Larreamendy-Joerns, Mary K. Stein, and Catherine A. Brown. "'You're Going to Want to Find Out Which and Prove It': Collective Argument in a Mathematics Classroom." *Learning and Instruction* 8, no. 6 (1998): 527–48.

Gallas, Karen. *Talking Their Way into Science: Hearing Children's Questions and Theories, Responding with Curricula.* New York: Teachers College Press, 1995.

Gallas, Karen, Mary Anton-Oldenberg, Cynthia Ballenger, Cindy Beseler, Steve Griffin, Roxanne Pappenheimer, and James Swaim. "Talking the Talk and Walking the Walk: Researching Oral Language in the Classroom." *Language Arts* 73 (1996): 608–17.

Gay, Geneva. *Culturally Responsive Teaching: Theory, Research, and Practice.* Multicultural Education Series. New York: Teachers College Press, 2000.

Grant, Maureen, and Rebecca McGraw. "Collaborating to Investigate and Improve Classroom Mathematics Discourse." In *Teachers Engaged in Research: Inquiry into Mathematics Classrooms, Grades 9–12,* edited by Laura Van Zoest, pp. 231–51. Greenwich, Conn.: Information Age Publishing, 2006. Available from National Council of Teachers of Mathematics.

Gutstein, Eric. *Reading and Writing the World with Mathematics: Toward a Pedagogy for Social Justice.* New York: Routledge, Taylor, & Francis Group, 2006.

Heath, Shirley B. *Ways with Words: Language, Life, and Work in Communities and Classrooms.* New York: Cambridge University Press, 1983.

Herbel-Eisenmann, Beth A. "Using Student Contributions and Multiple Representations to Develop Mathematical Language." *Mathematics Teaching in the Middle School* 8, no. 2 (October 2002):100–5.

Herbel-Eisenmann, Beth A., and M. Lynn Breyfogle. "Questioning Our *Patterns* of Questions." *Mathematics Teaching in the Middle School* 10, no. 9 (May 2005): 484–89.

Herbel-Eisenmann, Beth, Jean Krusi, Joe Obrycki, Jeffrey Marks, Lana Lyddon-Hatten, Patty Gronewald, Darin Dowling, Angie Shindelar, Tammie Cass, Michelle Cirillo, and Katie Skowronski. "What I Learned over My Summer Vacation about Classroom Discourse." Teachers of Teachers Research Session at the Annual Meeting of the National Council of Teachers of Mathematics, Atlanta, Georgia, March 22, 2007.

Huhn, Craig, Kellie Huhn, and Peg Lamb. "Lessons Teachers Can Learn about Students' Mathematical Understanding through Conversations with Them about Their Thinking: Implications for Practice." In *Teachers Engaged in Research: Inquiry into Mathematics Classrooms, Grades 9–12,* edited by Laura Van Zoest, pp. 97–118. Greenwich, Conn.: Information Age Publishing, 2006. Available from National Council of Teachers of Mathematics.

Kazemi, Elham, and Deborah Stipek. "Promoting Conceptual Thinking in Four Upper-Elementary Mathematics Classrooms." *Elementary School Journal* 102, no. 1 (2001): 59–80.

Lampert, Magdalene, and Paul Cobb. "Communication and Language." In *A Research Companion to* Principles and Standards for School Mathematics, edited by Jeremy Kilpatrick, W. Gary Martin, and Deborah Schifter, pp. 237–49. Reston, Va.: National Council of Teachers of Mathematics, 2003.

Lampert, Magdalene, Peggy Rittenhouse, and Carol Crumbaugh. "Agree to Disagree: Developing Sociable Mathematical Discourse in School." In *The Handbook of Education and Human Development: New Models of Learning, Teaching and Schooling,* edited by David Olson and Nancy Torrance, pp. 731–64. Oxford: Basil Blackwell, 1996.

Lee, Clare. *Language for Learning Mathematics: Assessment for Learning in Practice.* New York: Open University Press, 2006.

Lubienski, Sarah T. "A Clash of Social Class Cultures? Students' Experiences in a Discussion-Intensive Seventh-Grade Mathematics Classroom." *Elementary School Journal* 100, no. 4 (2000): 377–403.

Malloy, Carol E., and William W. Malloy. "Issues of Culture in Mathematics Teaching and Learning." *Urban Review* 30, no. 3 (1998): 245–57.

Mehan, Hugh. *Learning Lessons.* Cambridge, Mass: Harvard University Press, 1979.

Moschkovich, Judit. "Bilingual Mathematics Learners: How Views of Language, Bilingual Learners, and Mathematical Communication Affect Instruction." In *Improving Access to Mathematics: Diversity and Equity in the Classroom,* edited by Na'ilah Suad Nasir and Paul Cobb, pp. 121–44. New York: Teachers College Press, 2007.

National Council of Teachers of Mathematics (NCTM). *Curriculum and Evaluation Standards for School Mathematics.* Reston, Va.: NCTM, 1989

———. *Professional Standards for Teaching Mathematics.* Reston, Va.: NCTM, 1991.

———. *Principles and Standards for School Mathematics.* Reston, Va.: NCTM, 2000.

O'Connor, Mary C., and Sarah Michaels. "Aligning Academic Task and Participation Status through Revoicing: Analysis of a Classroom Discourse Strategy." *Anthropology and Education Quarterly* 24 (1993): 318–35.

———. "Shifting Participant Frameworks: Orchestrating Thinking Practices in Group Discussion." In *Discourse, Learning and Schooling*, edited by Deborah Hicks, pp. 63–103. New York: Cambridge University Press, 1996.

Reeves, Nancy. "Action Research for Professional Development: Informing Teachers and Researchers." In *Transforming Children's Mathematics Education*, edited by Leslie P. Steffe and Terry Wood. Hillsdale, N.J.: Lawrence Erlbaum Associates, 1990.

Rittenhouse, Peggy S, "The Teacher's Role in Mathematical Conversation: Stepping In and Stepping Out." In *Talking Mathematics in School: Studies of Teaching and Learning*, edited by Magdelene Lampert and Merrie L. Blink, pp. 163–89. New York: Cambridge University Press, 1998.

Schleppegrell, Mary J. *The Language of Schooling: A Functional Linguistics Perspective.* Mahwah, N.J.: Lawrence Erlbaum Associates, 2004.

———. "The Linguistic Challenges of Mathematics Teaching and Learning: A Research Review." *Reading and Writing Quarterly* 23 (2007):139–59.

Sfard, Anna. "On Reform Movement and the Limits of Mathematical Discourse." *Mathematical Thinking and Learning* 2, no. 3 (2000):157–89.

Sleeter, Christine. "Mathematics, Multicultural Education, and Professional Development." *Journal for Research in Mathematics Education* 28, no. 6 (December 1997): 680–96.

Stein, Mary K. "Mathematical Argumentation: Putting Umph into Classroom Discussions." *Mathematics Teaching in the Middle School* 7, no. 2 (October 2001): 110–12.

Stigler, James W., and James Hiebert. *The Teaching Gap.* New York: Free Press, 1999.

Thompson, Denise R., and Rheta N. Rubenstein. "Learning Mathematics Vocabulary: Potential Pitfalls and Instructional Strategies." *Mathematics Teacher* 93, no. 7 (October 2000): 568–74.

Toulmin, Stephen. *The Uses of Argument.* London: Cambridge University Press, 1958.

Warren, Beth, and Ann S. Rosebery. "Equity in the Future Tense: Redefining Relations among Teachers, Students, and Science in Linguistic Minority Classrooms." In *New Directions in Equity for Mathematics Education*, edited by Walter G. Secada, Elizabeth Fennema, and Lynda Byrd Adajian, pp. 298–328. New York: Cambridge University Press, 1995.

Wells, Gordon, ed. *Action, Talk, and Text: Learning and Teaching through Inquiry.* New York: Teachers College Press, 2001.

Wood, Terry. "Alternative Patterns of Communication in Mathematics Classes: Funneling or Focusing?" In *Language and Communication in the Mathematics Classroom*, edited by Heinz Steinbring, Maria G. Bartolini Bussi, and Anna Sierpinska, pp. 167–78. Reston, Va.: NCTM, 1998.

———. "Creating a Context for Argument in Mathematics Class." *Journal for Research in Mathematics Education* 30, no. 2 (March 1999):171–91.

Yackel, Erna, and Paul Cobb. "Sociomathematical Norms, Argumentation, and Autonomy in Mathematics." *Journal for Research in Mathematics Education* 27, no. 4 (July 1996): 458–77.

11

Discussions of Mathematical Thinking: Engaging All Students in Learning Mathematics

George W. Bright
Jeane M. Joyner

ONE OF the most important things a mathematics teacher can do is help students make sense of mathematics ideas. Sometimes sense making happens when students work alone on solving a problem, but more often it happens when students share and compare their work with peers. Discussing mathematical thinking is a crucial part of mathematics instruction. Not all teachers are equally good at leading such discussions, but all teachers can gain skill in this area through taking part in professional development sessions.

Leading effective discussions involves some "art" and some "science." Asking an engaging question is one way to begin effective discussions and to invite all students into the conversation. Such encouragement is especially important for students who do not see themselves as capable or successful learners of mathematics. Engaging questions are ones such as "How did you begin thinking about this problem?" or "What is something important you noticed in this problem?" Both these questions indicate that the teacher values the ideas of students and is interested in their thinking. Rather than begin by asking "What is the answer?"—a question that usually has only one correct response—a teacher can encourage the hesitant student to speak by asking a question for which a variety of responses may be appropriate.

Another factor is to keep students focused on essential ideas without straying too much from these central points. Of course, when an unexpected, but interesting, idea surfaces, it may need to be pursued. These unexpected events are often the "teachable moments" that every teacher has experienced. But knowing when to pursue and when to limit discussion requires a deep understanding of both the underlying mathematics and the ways that ideas develop in students' minds. The science of leading discussions, then, is in having this background and in keeping the big picture in mind during discussions. The art of leading discussions is in using that background to make on-the-fly decisions that support students in sense making.

As students share their thinking, teachers have opportunities to assess the state of students' learning. Teachers can identify the logic that students

> Asking an engaging question is one way to begin effective discussions and to invite all students into the conversation.

> Knowing when to pursue and when to limit discussion requires a deep understanding of both the underlying mathematics and the ways that ideas develop in students' minds.

The work reported here was supported in part by grant number 9819914 from the National Science Foundation. The opinions expressed are those of the authors and do not necessarily reflect the position of the Foundation or any other government agency.

117

are using, the ideas that students have internalized, the knowledge that is tentative and fragile for students, and the misunderstandings that students may have developed. Understanding what students know is part of the process that we call *classroom assessment* (Bright and Joyner 2004), that is, formative assessment designed to provide information to teachers so that instructional decisions are better aligned with students' needs. When classroom assessment is implemented effectively, it can change mathematics teaching and improve mathematics learning (Black et al. 2004; Black and Wiliam 1998a, 1998b; Bright and Joyner 2004–2005, 2006).

Usually students' responses to questions have a supporting "logic," although sometimes this logic is not mathematically correct. It may reflect students' perspectives of how the real world operates rather than how mathematical ideas are organized and connected. For example, students often incorrectly believe that if five heads have occurred in a row in the toss of a coin, then the probability of getting a tail is greater than one-half on the next toss to "balance" the total numbers of heads and tails. By revealing students' logic, teachers can help students understand how their perceptions of the world are consistent or inconsistent with mathematical knowledge.

Leading effective discussions is in many ways like conducting interviews. As part of listening to students in either setting, teachers make tentative hypotheses about what students do or do not understand, probe students' thinking to test those hypotheses, and pose questions to help students evaluate their own thinking. Also as in interviews, teachers make decisions ahead of time about what the goals of a discussion are—that is, what the learning targets are. Establishing clear learning targets is crucial for successful instruction and effective discussions. Students need to know what those learning targets are so they can monitor their progress toward attaining those targets. As learning targets are created, teachers need to identify the kinds of evidence that are acceptable indicators of having attained the intended learning. This evidence becomes part of what teachers look for during discussions.

Classroom Assessment and Learning

Learning how to implement classroom assessment takes time and effort, but evidence shows that when teachers incorporate classroom assessment into instruction and instructional planning— for example, by leading effective discussions— students benefit.

Learning how to implement classroom assessment takes time and effort, but evidence shows that when teachers incorporate classroom assessment into instruction and instructional planning—for example, by leading effective discussions—students benefit. As Wilson and Kenney (2003, p. 55) report,

> Black and Wiliam (1998) conclude from an examination of 250 research studies on classroom assessment that "formative assessment does improve learning"—and that the achievement gains are "among the largest ever reported for educational interventions." The effect size of 0.7, on average, illustrates just how large these gains are…. In other words, if mathematics teachers were to focus their efforts on classroom assessment that is primarily formative, students' learn-

ing gains would be impressive. These efforts would include gathering data through classroom questioning and discourse, using a variety of assessment tasks, and attending primarily to what students know and understand.

Probing students' thinking and attending to what students know and understand are crucial elements of leading effective discussions. As reported in Pellegrino, Chudowsky, and Glaser (2001, p. 38),

> According to the results of this review [i.e., Black and Wiliam 1998], students learn more when they receive feedback about particular qualities of their work, along with advice on what they can do to improve. They also benefit from training in self-assessment, which helps them understand the main goals of the instruction and determine what they need to do to achieve.

One of the payoffs of effective discussions is that students become more engaged in significant learning. Greater intellectual rigor becomes evident, partly because students are making sense of the mathematics and partly because students are learning how to be more reflective about their own learning. Unfortunately, intellectual rigor is not a hallmark of many lessons. "Fewer than 1 in 5 mathematics and science lessons are strong in intellectual rigor; include teacher questioning that is likely to enhance student conceptual understanding; and provide sense-making appropriate for the needs of the students and the purposes of the lesson" (Weiss et al. 2003, p. 103). Students are not likely to make sense of mathematics automatically. Discussions provide an environment in which sense making and intellectual rigor can happen.

Leading Discussions

Leading discussions is not always easy. Frequently, effective discussions occur around the debriefing of students' work on a significant task, so choosing a rich task that can generate discussion of students' thinking is an important precursor to the actual discussion. Task selection reflects teachers' personal understanding of mathematics. That is, the kinds of mathematics that a teacher views as important (e.g., concepts or procedures) influence both the choice of tasks and the questions used in follow-up discussions of those tasks. Below are some aspects of leading a discussion:

- *Asking an engaging question to begin the discussion.* As noted previously, engaging questions (Bright and Joyner 2004, p. 153) invite students into a discussion. Engaging questions typically have multiple appropriate answers, so students at different levels of mathematical understanding can respond acceptably. This openness tends to capture students' interest and motivates them to participate.

- *Deciding which student should respond to a question.* Often, teachers call on volunteers during discussions. This tactic has the effect of allowing students, rather than the teacher, to control the flow of information, that is, to decide what is important to say and what is important not to say. Since students are usually novices when learning new content, they cannot reasonably be expected to know what is most important or least important about the mathematics being discussed. Teachers can maintain control of the flow of information by knowing how students have solved the problem and by having students share those solutions that are most likely to help other students understand the essential mathematics ideas. Knowing what is likely to help a group of students collectively is especially important when diverse learners are present in a classroom.

- *Listening carefully to a student's response.* Teachers need to decide, sometimes quite quickly, what a student is "really" trying to say. Often, however, students do not have the language skills needed to communicate clearly what they are really thinking. Language skills go well beyond just knowing terminology. Students need to be able to explain their thinking, and doing so is often not easy. Teachers can help students by modeling a variety of different kinds of correct reasoning so that students have multiple ways to explain their thinking. In this approach, teachers need to listen for what the student is actually trying to say rather than what the teacher would like the student to say. Then, teachers can help students reorganize their language so that it accurately reflects their thinking.

- *Making inferences about what knowledge is revealed by a student's response.* Teachers need to decide what mathematics understanding is actually reflected in what a student says. Teachers should not put too much meaning into what students say, because such inferences can lead teachers to conclude that students know more than they actually do. A better choice may be to err on the side of inferring too little about what students understand rather than too much. Inferring too much may result in instruction that moves beyond what students are ready to internalize.

- *Asking follow-up questions to probe a student's thinking.* Teachers often ask very good questions, but they are not always confident about the quality of those questions. Being able to ask good probing and clarifying questions on-the-fly, without "scaffolding" students' responses with small step-by-step questions that lead students to an answer, is a skill that takes time to develop. Teachers also need to know when additional probing in the classroom setting becomes intimidating to some students, thus making less likely those students' willingness to speak up in the future.

- *Paraphrasing a student's response to be sure you understood the student's thinking.* Paraphrasing slows the pace of instruction and gives all students time to reflect on their own thinking and to judge whether their thinking is consistent with the response being paraphrased. Paraphrasing also gives the teacher a chance to reinforce correct terminology or perhaps to fill in a detail that might have been omitted in a student's response.

- *Summarizing the discussion.* Summarizing provides closure to a discussion, but it also gives students a chance to firm up their understanding of the mathematics that was discussed. Knowledge is not very useful until it is firmly integrated into one's mind. If instruction moves along too quickly, the fragile knowledge that students "seem" to have acquired can quickly dissipate.

Decision Making during Discussions

The process of debriefing of students' solutions to problems offers an excellent opportunity for teachers to make sense of students' thinking and to help students make sense of both their own thinking and the thinking of their peers. Let us examine this process in the context of one particular problem (adapted from Bright and Joyner 2004–2005, p. 11).

> Mrs. Allen took a 3-inch-by-5-inch photo of the Cape Hatteras Lighthouse and made an enlargement on a photocopier using the 200% option. Which is "more square," the photo or the copy?

As students work on the problem, you observe what they are doing, that is, the answers they generate and the strategies they use. Suppose you observe the solutions below. (These responses are adapted from responses of first-year algebra students. The language has been abbreviated to save space.)

Luanne	Carlos
photo: 3 by 5	photo: 3 by 5, difference is 2
copy: 6 by 10	enlargement: 6 by 10, difference is 4
3/5 and 6/10 are equal, so the pictures are equally square.	Photo has smaller difference, so it is more square.
Pat	**Chris**
photo: 3 by 5, difference is 2, and 2 out of 5 is 40%	photo: 3 × 5 = 15
copy: 6 by 10, difference is 4, and 4 out of 10 is 40%	copy: 6 × 10 = 60
Each pictures is 40% away from square, so they are equally square.	60 is more so the copy is more square.

Several concerns need to be accounted for in structuring the discussion of students' work for this problem: (1) determining solutions' correctness, (2) determining the mathematics thinking revealed by the solutions, (3) probing individual students' thinking, (4) choosing the solutions to share, and (5) determining the order in which those solutions are shared.

The first step in thinking about which solutions to discuss is deciding which ones are correct. When teachers plan, they often think about the correct and incorrect ways that students might solve a problem, so much of the decision making about correctness of students' responses is actually done prior to a lesson. Luanne solved the problem in the way that most teachers would say is correct; comparing the ratios of sides reflects the use of proportional reasoning in ways that most teachers want. Carlos approached the problem from an additive (rather than proportional reasoning) perspective; just computing differences of sides does not account for the relative sizes of the two figures. That is, Carlos used only part of the essential information. Pat also computed differences but then accounted for the relative sizes by comparing each difference with the length of the corresponding rectangle; this strategy was mathematically correct but may not have been easily understood by other students. Chris focused on area and generated an answer that involved mathematics that was inappropriate for this problem. The range of responses shown here illustrates the dilemma of all teachers, that of how we can deal with the needs of diverse learners. The range of mathematics understanding illustrated here is large, yet the teachers had to do their best to accommodate individual differences while teaching the class as a group.

Then we had to decide what each solution told us about that student's thinking. Luanne and Pat seemed to be thinking proportionally. Carlos perhaps did not understand proportional reasoning or perhaps did not realize that proportional reasoning applied to this problem. Chris was distracted by inappropriate mathematics; sometimes when students lack understanding of the appropriate mathematics, they "call up" mathematics that they are comfortable with, without determining whether it is appropriate for the problem.

As teachers watch students work, they find opportunities to probe students' thinking. Probing both correct and incorrect answers is important to help reveal students' deeper mathematics understanding.

- *To Luanne:* Why is it important that the ratios 3/5 and 6/10 are equal?

- *To Carlos:* Why is it helpful to compute the differences of the lengths and widths?

- *To Pat:* What do you mean when you say "40 percent away from square"?

- *To Chris:* Why is it helpful to compute the areas of the rectangles?

Teachers must understand how students think about important mathematics ideas. Each student is the "expert" on her or his own thinking, so when we want to know how a student is thinking, the most direct approach is to ask that student.

Then we have to decide which solutions to put in front of the class and which solutions to pass over, at least in public. In part this decision involves thinking about which solutions can help further the development of students' understanding of the underlying mathematics ideas. Sometimes a solution is too far "off" to be useful for discussion, and sometimes a solution is too sophisticated for the majority of students to grasp. Some teachers do not want students to see incorrect strategies; those teachers might choose to discuss only Luanne's and Pat's solutions. Other teachers believe that students can learn from seeing incorrect answers; these teachers might choose also to discuss Carlos' solution so that the error in the logic of this solution can be made explicit. Carlos' strategy was a very common one for students to apply, and Carlos was probably not the only one in the class to reason in the way he did. Knowing how many students are using a particular strategy is one of the criteria that can be used in deciding what strategies to share. Because Chris used inappropriate mathematics, many teachers might have chosen not to share that solution; the solution may have been "too far off." A teacher might, however, have decided to discuss Chris' solution in private to be sure that Chris understood why computing areas was not useful for this problem.

Teachers should carefully choose the solutions to share. Students can learn to be flexible in their thinking by listening to their peers explain different approaches to a problem and then discussing those approaches to determine which ones are correct and efficient. Managing the sharing of solutions for the purpose of helping all students develop deeper understanding of essential mathematics ideas is difficult but crucially important in creating effective instruction.

Finally, we have to decide the order in which to discuss the "public" solutions. Different choices might be made, and no single choice should be used exclusively. Any teaching technique that is used exclusively will tend to make instruction boring and predictable, and in fact, implicitly encourage students to stop thinking. Making a variety of choices across a range of problems will help keep students engaged in thinking about important mathematics ideas.

- *Incorrect solution first.* If a correct solution is shared first, then students who realize that their solutions are incorrect may not be willing to share them. Conversely, if an incorrect solution is shared first, the student who shared may begin to become defensive as the class reaches consensus that this solution is incorrect. Teachers can blunt these emotional issues by establishing the classroom norm that everyone can learn from mistakes, both their own and others'. Also, by identifying how an incorrect solution went "off track," students can reorganize their approaches to problem solving so as to avoid those traps. Knowing what does not work may be as important as knowing what does work.

- *Least sophisticated to most sophisticated, independent of correctness.* The primary advantage of this choice is that more students may remain involved in the discussion, just because they understand the reasoning that is being discussed. If a discussion begins with a sophisticated solution, students who do not understand it may "tune out" and may not be willing or able to re-engage in the discussion.

- *Ask for volunteers.* When we ask for volunteers, we are putting them in charge of choosing what information gets shared. Their choices may not be the best ones. Volunteers often come from a small group of students, too; this tendency may disenfranchise the remainder of a class.

- *Call on students randomly.* Sometimes teachers call on students in a more-or-less random fashion. The intent of this approach is to keep all students engaged, since they do not know when they might be chosen to respond. The disadvantage is that the teacher often does not know what students are going to say, and as a result, may lose control of the flow of information.

> **Managing the sharing of solutions for the purpose of helping all students develop deeper understanding of essential mathematics ideas is difficult but crucially important in creating effective instruction.**

123

- *Call on someone who has the correct answer.* This choice creates the appearance that the discussion is moving along, but it may leave behind those students who are not thinking "correctly."

When a problem has a wide range of solution strategies, we believe the best approach may be to begin with the less sophisticated solutions that you have chosen to share and move toward the more sophisticated ones. The wide range of solutions is likely to represent a wide range of understanding, so the challenge is to keep most of the students engaged during the debriefing. Beginning with the less sophisticated solutions increases the likelihood that students will be able to follow the explanations.

When the range of solutions is narrow, however, a more efficient approach may be to share the solution(s) that best illustrate the underlying mathematics ideas, regardless of the level of sophistication of those solutions. A narrow range of solutions may indicate that most students are at about the same level of understanding, so they should be able to follow whatever solution is presented.

Conclusions

Most mathematics problems usually require integration of a variety of concepts and procedures. Students' solutions will likely reflect misconceptions or confusions about these concepts and procedures. Teachers must understand the complexity of students' thinking so that a debriefing discussion can help students make sense of all the solutions that are shared. Helping students learn to share their mathematical understandings and thinking will also help students reflect on what they know. Discussions can help all students in a class benefit by allowing reflection on a variety of approaches to a problem. Students can learn to appreciate diversity in approaches to problem solving and can broaden their repertoires of problem-solving strategies.

Engaging all students in conversations about their mathematical thinking is an instructional technique that has the potential to increase students' learning. Such discussions are not always easy to promote and manage, and not all teachers are equally adept at leading them. Thinking about, and talking about, how to lead good discussions can help all teachers become better discussion leaders.

Teachers must understand the complexity of students' thinking so that a debriefing discussion can help students make sense of all the solutions that are shared. Helping students learn to share their mathematical understandings and thinking will also help students reflect on what they know.

REFERENCES

Black, Paul, Christine Harrison, Clare Lee, Bethan Marshall, and Dylan Wiliam. "Working inside the Black Box: Assessment for Learning in the Classroom." *Phi Delta Kappan* 86, no. 1 (2004): 9–21.

Black, Paul, and Dylan Wiliam. "Assessment and Classroom Learning." *Assessment in Education* 5 (1998a): 7–74.

———. "Inside the Black Box: Raising Standards through Classroom Assessment." *Phi Delta Kappan* 80, no. 2 (1998b): 139–44.

Bright, George W., and Jeane M. Joyner. *Dynamic Classroom Assessment: Linking Mathematical Understanding to Instruction in Middle Grades and High School: Core Program: Facilitator's Guide.* Vernon Hills, Ill.: ETA/Cuisenaire, 2004.

―――. *Dynamic Classroom Assessment: Linking Mathematical Understanding to Instruction in Middle Grades and High School: Revisiting Students' Understanding: Participant's Guide.* Vernon Hills, Ill.: ETA/Cuisenaire, 2005.

―――. "Classroom Assessment in Middle Grades and High School." *National Council of Supervisors of Mathematics Journal* 7, no. 2 (Fall-Winter 2004–2005): 11–17.

―――. "Improving Mathematics Instruction through Formative Classroom Assessment." *New England Mathematics Journal* 38, no. 2 (2006): 23–35.

Pellegrino, James W., Naomi Chudowsky, and Robert Glaser, eds. *Knowing What Students Know: The Science and Design of Educational Assessment.* Washington, D.C.: National Academy Press, 2001.

Weiss, Iris R., Joan D. Pasley, P. Sean Smith, Eric R. Banilower, and Dan J. Heck. *Looking inside the Classroom: A Study of K–12 Mathematics and Science Education in the United States.* Chapel Hill, N.C.: Horizon Research, 2003.

Wilson, Linda Dager, and Patricia Ann Kenney. "Classroom and Large-Scale Assessment." In *A Research Companion to* Principles and Standards for School Mathematics, edited by Jeremy Kilpatrick, W. Gary Martin, and Deborah Schifter, pp. 53–67). Reston, Va.: National Council of Teachers of Mathematics, 2003.

12

Learning from One Another: Why and How to Do Classroom Observations with Your Colleagues

Fran Arbaugh

IN THE other articles of this book, authors describe many instructional strategies that promote the learning of *all students*. I hope that as you read about those instructional strategies, you became motivated to try a few of them in your mathematics classroom. As a former high school mathematics teacher, I was often motivated to implement newly learned instructional strategies in my classroom, seeking those strategies that allowed me to involve all my students in the learning process. However, as much as I worked to incorporate new strategies into my teaching, I often felt dissatisfied when I could not really assess changes in my teaching and whether those changes prompted all my students—with all their different needs, talents, and learning styles—to be more involved in doing and reflecting on, and thus learning, mathematics. I was too close to the action to be able to take an objective view. Further, although I talked with colleagues in my department about the changes I was trying to make, they often could not see what I was doing in my class. I felt isolated and frustrated.

If only I had known then what I know now! In my position as a university mathematics teacher educator, I frequently work with area high school mathematics teachers. During one professional development project, the teachers formed study groups that met during the academic year. Three project teachers approached me with the idea of engaging in several observation-and-debriefing sessions in one another's classrooms during the upcoming year. These teachers believed that they could think more deeply about instructional strategies by learning from one another in the places where they do their work—in their classrooms. They wanted me to join the group, too, and play a participant-facilitator role.

How often do you, as a high school mathematics teacher, get to observe in a colleague's mathematics class and then spend time debriefing about what you observed? "What?" you might be saying to yourself. "Is she kidding? I barely have time to teach my own classes, much less observe in someone else's classroom." If this comment describes what you are thinking, you are not alone. High school mathematics teachers often work in isolated conditions, rarely collaborating with their colleagues about the mathematics they teach (Stigler and Hiebert 1999). The contact they do have with other teachers in their departments is often in the form of department meetings, in which the focus of discussion is most likely administrative concerns. High

> As much as I worked to incorporate new strategies into my teaching, I often felt dissatisfied when I could not really assess whether those changes prompted all my students—with all their different needs, talents, and learning styles—to be more involved in doing and reflecting on, and thus learning, mathematics.

> High school mathematics teachers often work in isolated conditions, rarely collaborating with their colleagues about the mathematics they teach (Stigler and Hiebert 1999).

127

school mathematics teachers may also share a common "planning" space, a department workroom or teacher-lunchroom space where teachers gather during the school day. In these places teachers share physical space while they often individually grade papers, write quizzes and tests, plan for upcoming lessons, or recoup energy before their next class. Grossman, Wineburg, and Woolworth (2001) write, "The simple fact is that the structures for ongoing community do not exist in the American high school" (p. 947).

This article is about a strategy that high school mathematics teachers can use to help create community and work collaboratively to differentiate and improve their classroom instruction to address the needs of all their students. The recommendations in this article come from two sources: (1) my and my teacher colleagues' experiences in our study group, when we completed several observation-and-debriefing cycles in the teachers' classrooms; and (2) a set of resources that we used to focus our observations and discussions. In the following sections, I first describe the mechanics of our study group and what the teachers said about participating in this type of professional development. I then make recommendations for starting such a study group in your school or district.

Our Study Group

Our study group met during the 2003–2004 school year. That year, Teresa, Lisa, and Rebecca taught in two different schools in the same midsized district (grades K–12 population 16,000). Teresa taught at a junior high school in grades 8–9; Lisa and Rebecca taught at the same high school in grades 10–12. When these teachers formed their study group, they did so on the basis of a common interest, not a common location. They believed that a difference in school settings would increase diversity in the group. In the summer before the school year began, we briefly met to set an initial meeting date; at that time we also made the decision to meet once a month during the school year, with our first two meetings being dedicated to arriving at consensus about our goals for the year.

Prior to our first meeting, I spent some time becoming familiar with a type of learning community called a *critical friends group*. I used the Web site of the National School Reform Faculty (NSRF) (www.nsrfharmony.org) to read about critical friends groups. I made copies of articles I found there to bring to the study group for discussion. The information on this Web site caused me to realize that we needed some kind of structure for our observations and debriefing sessions. The NSRF Web site also contained protocols that helped guide these types of activities.

Setting Goals

During our first study-group meeting, the teachers decided that they would like to focus our work together on teacher questioning during whole-class instruction. Each of the teachers was concerned that her questioning skills were not inclusive of *all students*, and that participating in this group would encourage them to become more focused on their questions and the types of responses that those questions elicited from their

The teachers wanted to become more focused on their questions and the types of responses that those questions elicited from their students.

students. As a consequence of this teacher-determined focus, we read a number of articles about questioning, including the three listed in figure 12.1. As we discussed these articles in our study group, our conversation returned to the teachers' goal for their questioning: they sought to be more inclusive of all students in their mathematics classrooms.

Mewborn, Denise S., and Patricia D. Huberty. "Questioning Your Way to the Standards." *Teaching Children Mathematics* 6 (December 1999): 226–27, 243–46.

Reinhardt, Steven C. "Never Say Anything a Kid Can Say." *Mathematics Teaching in the Middle School* 5 (April 2000): 478–83.

Sherin, Miriam G., Edith P. Mendez, and David A. Louis. "Talking about Math Talk." In *Learning Mathematics for a New Century,* 2000 Yearbook of the National Council of Teachers of Mathematics (NCTM), edited by Maurice J. Burke, pp. 188–96. Reston, Va.: NCTM, 2000.

Fig. 12.1. Three resources on questioning

We also read articles on critical friends groups and examined a number of protocols that could help guide our observation-and-debriefing cycles. The teachers agreed that they wanted this study group to reflect the characteristics of critical friends groups, as described in the articles mentioned (see fig.12.2). The protocol that we decided to use for our observations and debriefing is called *focus point* (see fig. 12.3). Teresa, Lisa, and Rebecca each expressed that this protocol seemed "safe" to them. They were understandably a bit nervous about being observed by members of the group. Although the four of us had built a level of trust through working together during the first year of the professional development project, Lisa, Teresa, and Rebecca appreciated that this protocol would allow us to focus the observations and debriefing session on one aspect of their instruction—questioning.

Critical friends groups are designed to—
- create a professional learning community;
- make teaching practice explicit and public by "talking about teaching";
- help people involved in schools work collaboratively in democratic, reflective communities (Bambino 2002);
- establish a foundation for sustained professional development based on a spirit of inquiry (Silva 2002);
- provide a context to understand our work with students, our relationships with peers, and our thoughts, assumptions, and beliefs about teaching and learning;
- help educators help one another turn theories into practice and standards into actual student learning; and
- improve teaching and learning.

Fig. 12.2. Characteristics of a critical friends group
(adapted from www.nsrfharmony.org/faq.html#1)

Observation Protocol #2: Focus Point

This protocol is designed to help deepen the observed's understanding of his or her practice. The observer(s)' role is to note those events that relate to a particular aspect of the observed's practice and to then act as an active listener as the observed attempts to make sense of those events.

Preobservation Conference: In addition to outlining what will be occurring during the observation, the person to be observed asks the observer(s) to focus on a particular aspect of her or his practice. *Example:* "Would you look at how I respond to students' questions?"

Observation: The observer(s) focus on that aspect of practice raised during the preobservation conference. Field notes include both descriptions of "focus" events and related questions that the observer may wish to raise during the debriefing. The observer(s) may also wish to note events and questions outside the focus of the observation, but these may or may not be discussed during the debriefing.

Debriefing: The observer(s) begin by restating the focus and asking the observed to share her thoughts. *Example:* "What did you notice about how you responded to students' questions?" As the observed talks, the observer(s) (1) supply specific events that either corroborate or contrast with the observed's statements, (2) summarize what the observed is saying, (3) ask clarifying questions, and (4) raise questions related to the focus that were noted during the observation.

Note: Events and questions not directly related to the focus of the observation should be raised only after asking for permission from the observed, and some practitioners think even asking for permission is inappropriate. The observer(s) should refrain from stating their ideas and perspective on the issues unless specifically invited to do so. An important principle in this process is that at all times the person who is being observed is the one who is in control of the situation.

Fig. 12.3. Focus Point protocol
(adapted from www.nsrfharmony.org/protocol/peer_observation.htm)

Observing and Debriefing

We followed the same organization every time we did an observation-and-debriefing cycle. We met at the observed teacher's school thirty minutes before the scheduled observation. During that time, we had a preobservation meeting, during which the observed teacher told the rest of us what she would like us to focus on during the observation. Then we observed for one class period, taking field notes on the designated focus. After the observation, we met for about an hour, debriefing what happened during the observation.

According to the Focus Point protocol, the observed teacher begins by talking about the focus issue—in this instance, questioning. The following is the opening part of Lisa's debriefing session, in which she reflected on how she asks what she calls "rhetorical" questions.

Fran: So, how do you think it went? The observation protocol says that the observers begin by restating the focus and asking the observed to share her thoughts. For example, how do you think your questioning went? What do you feel about it?

Lisa: Umm, … I had some rhetorical questions.

Rebecca: What do you mean by *rhetorical?*

Lisa: I did have some questions that the whole class felt like they were just supposed to respond rhetorically. Like when I say, "So then we end up with $2x$ times $3x$, which is …?" Part of that is conditioning, because a lot of times we just do it that way and that is OK. It is like when I get to the end of my question, you know the way I'm saying this, and they are all just going to blurt it out.

Fran: Uh huh.

Lisa: And what do I do to prevent that from happening? It seems like I usually think that I have to do it at the beginning of the question: "Okay now, I want you to think about this," and if I haven't already set that stage and am in the middle of my question, I know I am sunk already. Students are just going to shout out an answer.

Rebecca: Right.

Lisa: So I don't know how much of that is just OK; it is part of how it is going to happen, and it is OK. It is not a big deal. Or is that something that I really need to, … um, I know it is bad if it happens all the time. If it is happening a little bit, is that OK, or is that something that I really need to work on? And then if so, how do I fix it when I am in the middle of a sentence and realize I haven't set it up correctly?

Lisa's opening statements were followed by the rest of us helping Lisa reflect more deeply on her questioning during this class. In our field notes we found instances in which Lisa had asked questions that encouraged more depth of thought from her students, and we prompted Lisa to reflect on those questions and what we had read in the articles about questioning. We then asked Lisa about other aspects of her questioning during the class, and focused our remaining discussions around her chosen topics.

Working to avoid rhetorical questions is a differentiating strategy that helps many different students participate in whole-class discussions. For example, when a teacher asks a rhetorical question, students who need a little more time to think about the question are left out when other students blurt out the answer. Although all the students may seem to be

Working to avoid rhetorical questions is a differentiating strategy that helps many different students participate in whole-class discussions.

answering at the same time, often in what is called a *choral answer*, usually the same group of students calls out each time. Also, students who want to elaborate on their answers, make verbal connections, or see mathematical relationships in a different way are more encouraged to participate when the teacher asks the kind of questions that encourage depth of thought from students. The types of questions that invite participation from students who are typically left out when a teacher asks rhetorical questions benefit all students.

We also did a second kind of observation-and-debriefing session during the year. Occasionally we would observe in someone's classroom that was not in the study group. We would then meet with that teacher to debrief what we had observed. We observed three different teachers at the high school level. Rebecca, Lisa, and Teresa chose three teachers that they wanted to observe; they focused on the observed teacher's questioning in each observation. We used a different protocol for these observations—the Interesting Moments protocol (see fig. 12.4).

Teachers' Reflections

At the end of each debriefing, I asked Rebecca, Lisa, and Teresa to reflect in writing about what they learned as either the observed or the observer during the observation-and-debriefing cycle. The following quotes come from their writing.

Observation Protocol #3: Interesting Moments

The underlying assumption for this protocol is that the observer and the observed will work together to create some new knowledge—they are in it together. The observation is a shared experience, and so is the debriefing. One outsider, after listening to such a debriefing, stated that it was a seamless conversation. "The two of you were discovering something about the events you had seen."

Preobservation Conference: Because this form of observation is more open-ended, a preconference is not strictly necessary, although it may help orient the observer as to what will be happening.

Observation: The observer maintains an open field of vision, noting anything that strikes her as particularly interesting—anything that may lead to "deep" questions.

Debriefing: Either participant begins by raising a point of interest, stating as clearly and as fully as possible what occurred. A conversation develops around the incident, with both observer and observed attempting to sort out "What was going on there?" As the ideas build, both are responsible for keeping the conversation on track while maintaining the flexibility necessary to create new understandings.

Note: Prerequisite for this protocol is a high level of trust between the two participants: trust that the debriefing is not about evaluation; trust that each will be thoughtful, will listen and respond to the other; trust that whatever knowledge is created will be shared knowledge.

Fig. 12.4. The Interesting Moments protocol
(adapted from www.nsrfharmony.org/protocol/peer_observation.html)

- *Rebecca* (after she was observed): I feel better now that it's over and I realize I am doing some things well. The debriefing time was extremely helpful to me, both in highlighting things that I could improve and things that are going well.

- *Lisa* (after observing Rebecca): First of all, I benefit greatly from being in the classroom of another teacher. It is good for me! I benefit as a teacher, especially since our area of focus [questioning] is all the same. It makes me realize that I am falling back into old habits.

- *Teresa* (after observing Pam, a veteran teacher): I feel that the purpose of observing another teacher, a master, is to learn different ways to manage and facilitate learning in a problems-based curriculum. I realized that it is possible to turn a classroom over to kids and still guide learning. I would like to take myself out of the front of the classroom and work on *not* giving kids answers.

Creating a Study Group with Your Colleagues

Creating and sustaining this kind of study group takes commitment to a common goal—for our group, improving the teachers' questioning with a focus on including all students in mathematical discussions. If you are interested in engaging in this kind of activity with colleagues, then these suggestions may be helpful to you:

1. *Choose a common goal.* All the members of the group should discuss and come to a consensus about a common goal to guide the group. We chose questioning as our focus; however, other strategies to differentiate instruction aimed at improving mathematical opportunities for all students also exist. Teachers can focus on offering students multiple options to take in information, to make sense of ideas, and to express what they have learned. Teachers can focus on providing different avenues for students to acquire content, to process ideas, or to develop products so that each student can learn effectively (Tomlinson 2001). Several strategies to differentiate instruction in mathematics are included in this book.

2. *Learn something new.* Our agreed-on goal was to focus on questioning. The teachers read articles about questioning to strengthen their own knowledge base and so that we could have a common language with which to talk about questioning in our debriefing sessions. No matter what instructional strategy you choose, learning something new about that strategy will likely enhance your experiences as you work to improve your classroom practices.

3. *Plan on the observation-and-debriefing cycle taking about one-half of a school day.* The preobservation meeting lasts about thirty minutes; the observation lasts about an hour; the debriefing lasts about an hour. With time to transition from activity to activity, we found that the cycle takes about three hours to complete.

I realized that it is possible to turn a classroom over to kids and still guide learning. I would like to take myself out of the front of the classroom and work on *not* giving kids answers.

No matter what instructional strategy you choose, learning something new about that strategy will likely enhance your experiences as you work to improve your classroom practices.

133

4. *Enlist the support of your administrator.* The teachers in our study group were supported through grant monies with a half-day substitute teacher. If you are not in the position to use that type of arrangement, garnering the support of your administrator will be essential to secure the time needed to engage in this process.

5. *Use a conversation guide.* The debriefing protocols that we used from the NSRF helped us focus our conversations and to be critical friends with one another. NSRF is not the only project that has created these types of conversation guides. The use of specific resources is not important; the important thing is to find a conversation guide that your group members are comfortable using.

6. *Limit the number of colleagues in a group.* We found that four was a good number for observations and debriefing. However, we could envision that this process would work with as few as three teachers and as many as six teachers.

Concluding Remarks

Research on teachers' education has long indicated that learning is enhanced when teachers engage in meaningful experiences with their colleagues (Little 1987, 1990; Loucks-Horsley et al. 2003). Working alone to improve your teaching can be discouraging. Establishing an observation-and-debriefing study group with your colleagues can enhance your experience as you work to incorporate new instructional strategies that promote learning for all students in your classroom.

REFERENCES

Bambino, Deborah. "Critical Friends." *Educational Leadership* 59, no. 6 (March 2002): 25–27.

Grossman, Pamela, Samuel Wineburg, and Stephen Woolworth. "Toward a Theory of Teacher Community." *Teachers College Record* 103 (December 2001): 942–1012.

Little, Judith W. "Teachers as Colleagues." In *Educator's Handbook: A Research Perspective*, edited by Virginia Richardson-Koehler, pp. 491–518. New York: Longman, 1987.

———. "The Persistence of Privacy: Autonomy and Initiative in Teachers' Professional Relations." *Teachers College Record* 91(Summer 1990): 509–36.

Loucks-Horsley, Susan, Nancy Love, Katherine E. Stiles, and Susan E. Mundry. *Designing Professional Development for Teachers of Science and Mathematics*. 2nd ed. Thousand Oaks, Calif.: Corwin Press, 2003.

Silva, Peggy. "What If …." *Connections: Journal of the National School Reform Faculty* (Spring 2002): 6, 14.

Stigler, James W., and James Hiebert. *The Teaching Gap: Best Ideas from the World's Teachers for Improving Education in the Classroom*. New York: Free Press, 1999.

Tomlinson, Carol Ann. *How to Differentiate Instruction in Mixed-Ability Classrooms*. 2d ed. Alexandria, Va.: Association for Supervision and Curriculum Development, 2001.

Two additional titles appear in the
Mathematics for Every Student
series

(Carol E. Malloy, series editor):

- ***Mathematics for Every Student: Responding to Diversity, Grades Pre-K–5,*** edited by Dorothy Y. White and Julie Sliva Spitzer

- ***Mathematics for Every Student: Responding to Diversity, Grades 6–8,*** edited by Mark W. Ellis

Please consult www.nctm.org/catalog for the availability of these titles, as well as for a plethora of resources for teachers of mathematics at all grade levels.

For the most up-to-date listing of NCTM resources on topics of interest to mathematics educators, as well as information on membership benefits, conferences, and workshops, visit the NCTM Web site at www.nctm.org.